Free Video  Free Video

Essential Test Tips Video from Trivium Test Prep

Dear Customer,

Thank you for purchasing from Trivium Test Prep! We're honored to help you prepare for your PSB HOAE exam.

To show our appreciation, we're offering a **FREE *PSB HOAE Essential Test Tips* Video by Trivium Test Prep.*** Our video includes 35 test preparation strategies that will make you successful on the PSB HOAE. All we ask is that you email us your feedback and describe your experience with our product. Amazing, awful, or just so-so: we want to hear what you have to say!

To receive your **FREE *PSB HOAE Essential Test Tips* Video**, please email us at 5star@triviumtestprep.com. Include "Free 5 Star" in the subject line and the following information in your email:

1. The title of the product you purchased.
2. Your rating from 1 – 5 (with 5 being the best).
3. Your feedback about the product, including how our materials helped you meet your goals and ways in which we can improve our products.
4. Your full name and shipping address so we can send your **FREE *PSB HOAE Essential Test Tips* Video**.

If you have any questions or concerns please feel free to contact us directly at 5star@triviumtestprep.com.

Thank you!

- Trivium Test Prep Team

*To get access to the free video please email us at 5star@triviumtestprep.com, and please follow the instructions above.

PSB HEALTH OCCUPATIONS STUDY GUIDE 2019 – 2020

Nursing Exam Prep Book and Practice Test Questions for the PSB HOAE (Health Occupations Aptitude Exam)

TABLE OF CONTENTS

ONLINE RESOURCES

To help you fully prepare for your Health Occupation Aptitude Examination (HOAE), Ascencia includes online resources with the purchase of this study guide.

PRACTICE TEST

In addition to the practice test included in this book, we also offer an online exam. Since many exams today are computer based, getting to practice your test-taking skills on the computer is a great way to prepare.

FLASH CARDS

A convenient supplement to this study guide, Ascencia's flash cards enable you to review important terms easily on your computer or smartphone.

CHEAT SHEETS

Review the core skills you need to master the exam with easy-to-read Cheat Sheets.

FROM STRESS TO SUCCESS

Watch "From Stress to Success," a brief but insightful YouTube video that offers the tips, tricks, and secrets experts use to score higher on the exam.

REVIEWS

Leave a review, send us helpful feedback, or sign up for Ascencia promotions—including free books!

Access these materials at:

www.ascenciatestprep.com/psb-hoae-online-resources

INTRODUCTION

What is the HOAE?

The Health Occupation Aptitude Examination (HOAE) was developed by the Psychological Services Bureau (PSB) for use by health care education programs during the application process. The exam evaluates candidates' relevant knowledge and skills so that they can be accurately placed in health care education programs. The HOAE is taken by candidates looking to begin coursework relevant to a wide range of health care positions, including:

+ practical nurse
+ therapy assistant
+ radiology technician
+ dental hygienist
+ pharmacy technician
+ veterinary technician
+ paramedic/EMT

What's on the HOAE?

The HOAE is a multiple-choice test that includes concepts covered in eighth-grade–level English, math, and science classes. The exam will also test your ability to identify relationships between shapes and includes a short vocational test designed to measure your personal suitability to work in health care.

HOAE Content			
Test	**Concepts**	**Number of Questions**	**Time**
Part I: Academic Aptitude	**Verbal Subtest**: identifying related vocabulary words	75	40 minutes
	Arithmetic Subtest: performing arithmetic calculations		
	Nonverbal Subtest: identifying patterns in shapes		
Part II: Spelling Test	identifying misspelled words	45	15 minutes
Part III: Reading Comprehension	answering questions about the content of short passages	35	35 minutes
Part IV: Information in the Natural Sciences	answering questions about biology, chemistry, physics, and health	60	25 minutes
Part V: Vocational Adjustment Index	choosing to agree or disagree with statements about your personality and workplace behaviors	90	15 minutes
Total		**305 questions**	**2 hours and 10 minutes**

How is the HOAE Administered?

The HOAE is administered by individual health care education programs. Most programs will require that you take the test at a specified testing location, usually on their campus. You should check with the program to which you are applying to find their testing dates and locations. If you want to report your HOAE score to a school at which you did not test, you will need to contact the school's admissions office.

Before you take the HOAE, carefully check the policies and procedures for your particular test site. Fees and payment methods will vary by school. In addition, most schools will have specific requirements for what you will need to bring (e.g., identification, pencils) and what not to bring (e.g., calculators, cell phones).

The PSB allows you to re-take the HOAE. However, each school will have its own policy about which scores they will accept. Keep in mind that schools may require that you take the HOAE the same year that you are applying.

How is the HOAE Scored?

You will receive a raw score and a percentile rank for each of the five tests and three subtests. The raw score will simply show how many questions you answered correctly. The percentile rank will show how you scored compared to other candidates. For example, if you are in the seventy-fifth percentile for the Reading Comprehension test, that means you scored higher than 75 percent of all test takers. If you test at the health care education program to which you are applying, they will be sent a copy of your results.

There is no set "passing" score for the HOAE. Each program will have its own guidelines for how it interprets your scores during the application review process. Contact your school's admissions office if you would like to learn more about how they use HOAE score reports.

Ascencia Test Prep

With health care fields such as nursing, pharmacy, emergency care, and physical therapy becoming the fastest-growing industries in the United States, individuals looking to enter the health care industry or rise in their field need high-quality, reliable resources. Ascencia Test Prep's study guides and test preparation materials are developed by credentialed industry professionals with years of experience in their respective fields. Ascencia recognizes that health care professionals nurture bodies and spirits, and save lives. Ascencia Test Prep's mission is to help health care workers grow.

ONE: WORD KNOWLEDGE

The thirty verbal questions on the Academic Aptitude test will gauge your knowledge of common vocabulary words. You will see a list of five words labeled *a* through *e*, and your job is to find the word that doesn't fit with the others.

> **Verbal Question Format**
>
> *Which word is most different in meaning from the other words?*
>
> **1.** a. kind b. gracious c. friendly d. vicious e. considerate

Fortunately, to answer these questions, you don't have to know the exact definition of all the words. Usually you'll just need to pick out the word that doesn't match in tone. Having a large vocabulary will obviously help with these questions, but you can also use root words and affixes to determine the meaning of unfamiliar words.

Word Structure

An unfamiliar word itself can provide clues about its meaning. Most words consist of discrete pieces that determine their meaning; these pieces include word roots, prefixes, and suffixes.

Word roots are the bases from which many words take their form and meaning. The most common word roots are Greek and Latin, and a broad knowledge of these roots can make it much easier to determine the meaning of words.

Table 1.1. Common Word Roots

Root	Meaning	Examples
alter	other	alternate
ambi	both	ambidextrous
ami, amic	love	amiable
amphi	both ends, all sides	amphibian

Table 1.1. Common Word Roots (continued)

Root	Meaning	Examples
aqua	water	aqueduct
aud	to hear	audience
auto	self	autobiography
bell	war	belligerent
bene	good	benevolent
bio	life	biology
ced	yield, go	secede
chron	time	chronological
circum	around	circumference
contra, counter	against	contradict
crypt	hidden	cryptic
curr, curs, cours	to run	precursory
dict	to say	dictator
dyna	power	dynamic
dys	bad, hard, unlucky	dysfunctional
equ	equal, even	equanimity
fort	strength	fortitude
fract	to break	fracture
grad, gress	step	progression
graph	writing	graphic
hetero	different	heterogeneous
homo	same	homogenous
hypo	below, beneath	hypothermia
ject	throw	projection
logy	study of	biology
luc	light	elucidate
mal	bad	malevolent
meta, met	behind, between	metacognition
mis, miso	hate	misanthrope
morph	form, shape	morphology
mort	death	mortal
multi	many	multiple
path	feeling, disease	apathy

Root	Meaning	Examples
phil	love	philanthropist
port	carry	transportation
pseudo	false	pseudonym
psycho	soul, spirit	psychic
rupt	to break	disruption
sect, sec	to cut	section
sequ, secu	follow	consecutive
soph	wisdom, knowledge	philosophy
tele	far off	telephone
terr	earth	terrestrial
therm	heat	thermal
vent, vene	to come	convene

Prefixes

In addition to understanding the base of a word, it's helpful to know common affixes that change the meaning of words and demonstrate their relationships to other words. **Prefixes** are added to the beginning of words and frequently change their meaning (sometimes even to the opposite meaning).

Table 1.2. Common Prefixes

Prefix	Meaning	Examples
a, an	without, not	anachronism
ab, abs, a	apart, away from	abnormal
ad	toward	adhere
ante	before	anterior
anti	against	antipathy
bi	two	binary
circum	around	circumnavigate
di	two, double	diatomic
dia	across, through	dialectic
dis	not, apart	disenfranchise
ego	I, self	egomaniac
epi	upon, over	epigram, epiphyte
ex	out	extraneous

Table 1.2. Common Prefixes (continued)

Prefix	Meaning	Examples
ideo	idea	ideology
in, im	not	immoral
inter	between	interstellar
locus	place	locality
macro	large	macrophage
micro	small	micron
mono	one, single	monocle
poly	many	polygamy
pre	before	prescient
sym	with	symbiosis
un	not	unsafe

Suffixes

Suffixes are added to the end of words, and like prefixes they modify the meaning of the word root. Suffixes also serve an important grammatical function and can change a part of speech or indicate if a word is plural or related to a plural.

Table 1.3. Common Suffixes

Suffix	Meaning	Examples
able, ible	able, capable	visible
age	act of, state of, result of	wreckage
an, ian	native of, relating to	vegetarian
ance, ancy	action, process, state	defiance
ary, ery, ory	relating to, quality, place	aviary
cian	possessing a specific skill or art	physician
cule, ling	very small	sapling
cy	action, function	normalcy
dom	quality, realm	wisdom
ee	one who receives the action	nominee
en	made of, to make	silken
ence, ency	action, state of, quality	urgency
er, or	one who, that which	professor

Suffix	Meaning	Examples
escent	in the process of	adolescent
esis, osis	action, process, condition	neurosis
fic	making, causing	specific
ful	full of	frightful
hood	order, condition, quality	adulthood
ice	condition, state, quality	malice
ile	relating to, suited for, capable of	juvenile
ine	nature of	feminine
ion, sion, tion	act, result, state of	contagion
ish	origin, nature, resembling	impish
ism	system, manner, condition, characteristic	capitalism
ist	one who, that which	artist
ite	nature of, quality of, mineral product	graphite
ity, ty	state of, quality	captivity
ive	causing, making	exhaustive
ment	act of, state of, result	containment
some	like, apt, tending to	gruesome
tude	state of, condition of	aptitude
ure	state of, act, process, rank	rupture
y	inclined to, tend to	faulty

CONTINUE

Test Your Knowledge

Which word is most different in meaning from the other words?

1.	a. malice	b. hatred	c. animosity	d. hostility	e. sympathy
2.	a. condense	b. augment	c. boost	d. enlarge	e. expand
3.	a. serene	b. peaceful	c. agitated	d. tranquil	e. quiet
4.	a. bellow	b. shout	c. howl	d. whimper	e. shriek
5.	a. cease	b. persist	c. continue	d. remain	e. endure
6.	a. flourish	b. prosper	c. thrive	d. shrivel	e. multiply
7.	a. obscured	b. apparent	c. evident	d. clear	e. obvious
8.	a. sparse	b. plentiful	c. scant	d. meager	e. thin
9.	a. concur	b. agree	c. oppose	d. approve	e. unite
10.	a. deadly	b. benign	c. lethal	d. fatal	e. harmful

CONTINUE

ANSWER KEY

1. e.

Sympathy means "feeling pity or understanding for somebody"; the other four words describe negative emotions.

2. a.

Condense means to "make smaller or more compact," and the other four words mean to make larger.

3. c.

Agitated means disturbed or upset, and the other four words describe the feeling of being calm.

4. d.

Whimper means to "make a low whining sound," and the other four words describe making loud sounds.

5. a.

Cease means stop, and the other four words mean to keep going.

6. d.

Shrivel means shrink, and the other four words mean to become larger or better.

7. a.

Obscured means "to be hidden," and the other four words describe things that can be easily seen.

8. b.

Plentiful means "present in large amounts," and the other four words describe a small supply.

9. c.

Oppose means "go against," and the other four words mean to agree or go along with.

10. b.

Benign means "harmless," and the other four words describe something dangerous.

TWO: ARITHMETIC

The twenty arithmetic questions will require you to read word problems and perform calculations to find the answer. You will not be able to use a calculator.

Arithmetic Question Format

1. A nurse has 25 patients to see in a day. If she has seen 13 patients, how many patients still need to be seen?

   a. 7 b. 8 c. 12 d. 13 e. 38

Mathematical Operations

The four basic arithmetic operations are addition, subtraction, multiplication, and division.

+ **Add** to combine two quantities (6 + 5 = 11).
+ **Subtract** to find the difference of two quantities (10 − 3 = 7).
+ **Multiply** to add a quantity multiple times (4 × 3 = 12).
+ **Divide** to find out how many times one quantity goes into another (10 ÷ 2 = 5).

On the exam, operations questions will often be word problems. These problems will contain **clue words** that help you determine which operation to use.

Table 2.1. Operations Word Problems

Operation	Clue Words	Example
Addition	sum, together, (in) total, all, in addition, increased, give	Leslie has 3 pencils. If her teacher **gives** her 2 pencils, how many does she now have **in total**? 3 + 2 = 5 pencils

Table 2.1. Operations Word Problems (continued)

Operation	Clue Words	Example
Subtraction	minus, less than, take away, decreased, difference, How many left?, How many more/less?	Sean has 12 cookies. His sister **takes** 2 cookies. **How many** cookies does Sean have **left**? 12 − 2 = 10 cookies
Multiplication	product, times, of, each/ every, groups of, twice	A hospital department has 10 patient rooms. If **each** room holds 2 patients, how many patients can stay in the department? 10 × 2 = 20 patients
Division	divided, per, each/every, distributed, average, How many for each?, How many groups?	A teacher has 150 stickers to **distribute** to her class of 25 students. If each student gets the same number of stickers, **how many** stickers will **each** student get? 150 ÷ 25 = 6 stickers

PRACTICE QUESTIONS

1. A case of powder-free nitrile gloves contains 10 boxes. Each box contains 150 gloves. How many gloves are in the case?

    Answer:

    Multiply the number of boxes by the number of gloves in each box to find the total number of gloves.

    10 × 150 = **1500 gloves**

2. A taxi company charges $5 for the first mile traveled, then $1 for each additional mile. What is the cost of a 10-mile taxi ride?

    Answer:

    The first mile will cost $5, and the additional 9 miles will cost $1 each.

    cost = $5 + (9)($1) = **$14**

Operations with Positive and Negative Numbers

Positive numbers are greater than zero, and **negative numbers** are less than zero. Use the rules in Table 2.2 to determine the sign of the answer when performing operations with positive and negative numbers.

Helpful Hint: Subtracting a negative number is the same as adding a positive number:
$5 - (-10) = 5 + (+10) = 5 + 10 = 15$

Table 2.2. Operations with Positive and Negative Numbers

Addition and Subtraction	Multiplication and Division
positive + positive = positive $4 + 5 = 9$	positive × positive = positive $5 × 3 = 15$
negative + negative = negative $-4 + -5 = -9 \rightarrow -4 - 5 = -9$	negative × negative = positive $-6 × -5 = 30$
negative + positive = sign of the larger number $-15 + 9 = -6$	negative × positive = negative $-5 × 4 = -20$

A **number line** shows numbers increasing from left to right (usually with zero in the middle). When adding positive and negative numbers, a number line can be used to find the sign of the answer. When adding a positive number, count to the right; when adding a negative number, count to the left. Note that adding a negative value is the same as subtracting.

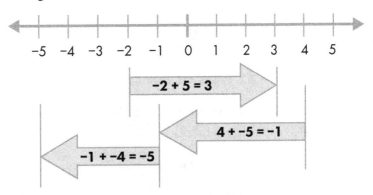

Figure 2.1. Adding Positive and Negative Numbers

PRACTICE QUESTION

The wind chill on a cold day in January was −3°F. When the sun went down, the temperature fell 5 degrees. What was the temperature after the sun went down?

<u>Answer:</u>

Because the temperature went down, add a negative number.

$-3 + -5 = \mathbf{-8°F}$

Fractions

A **fraction** represents parts of a whole. The top number of a fraction, called the **numerator**, indicates how many equal-sized parts are present. The bottom number of a fraction, called the **denominator**, indicates how many equal-sized parts make a whole.

Fractions have several forms:

+ **proper fraction**: the numerator is less than the denominator
+ **improper fraction**: the numerator is greater than or equal to the denominator
+ **mixed number**: the combination of a whole number and a fraction

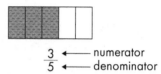

Figure 2.2. Parts of Fractions

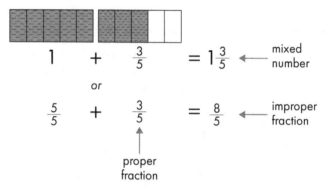

Figure 2.3. Types of Fractions

Improper fractions can be converted to mixed numbers by dividing. In fact, the fraction bar is also a division symbol.

$$\frac{14}{3} = 14 \div 3 = 4 \text{ (with 2 left over)}$$

$$\frac{14}{3} = 4\frac{2}{3}$$

To convert a mixed number to a fraction, multiply the whole number by the denominator of the fraction, and add the numerator. The result becomes the numerator of the improper fraction; the denominator remains the same.

$$5\frac{2}{3} = \frac{(5 \times 3) + 2}{3} = \frac{17}{3}$$

To **multiply fractions**, multiply numerators and multiply denominators. Reduce the product to lowest terms. To **divide fractions**, multiply the dividend (the first fraction) by the reciprocal of the divisor (the fraction that follows the division symbol).

When multiplying and dividing mixed numbers, the mixed numbers must be converted to improper fractions.

Helpful Hint: The reciprocal of a fraction is just the fraction with the top and bottom numbers switched.

Adding or subtracting fractions requires a common denominator. To find a **common denominator**, multiply the denominators of the fractions. Then, to add the fractions, add the numerators and keep the denominator the same.

PRACTICE QUESTIONS

1. $7\frac{1}{2} \times 1\frac{5}{6} =$

Answer:

Convert the mixed numbers to improper fractions.

$7\frac{1}{2} = \frac{7 \times 2 + 1}{2} = \frac{15}{2}$

$1\frac{5}{6} = \frac{1 \times 6 + 5}{6} = \frac{11}{6}$

Multiply the numerators, multiply the denominators, and reduce.

$\frac{15}{2} \times \frac{11}{6} = \frac{165}{12} = \frac{165 \div 3}{12 \div 3} = \mathbf{\frac{55}{4}}$

2. Ari and Teagan each ordered a pizza. Ari has $\frac{1}{4}$ of his pizza left, and Teagan has $\frac{1}{3}$ of her pizza left. How much total pizza do they now have?

Answer:

The common denominator is $4 \times 3 = 12$.

Convert each fraction to the common denominator.

$\frac{1}{4}\left(\frac{3}{3}\right) = \frac{3}{12}$

$\frac{1}{3}\left(\frac{4}{4}\right) = \frac{4}{12}$

Add the numerators and keep the denominator the same.

$\frac{3}{12} + \frac{4}{12} = \frac{7}{12}$

Together, they have $\mathbf{\frac{7}{12}}$ **of a pizza**.

Decimals

In the base-10 system, each digit (the numeric symbols 0 – 9) in a number is worth ten times as much as the number to the right of it. For example, in the number 321 each digit has a different value based on its location: 321 = 300 + 20 + 1. The value of each place is called **place value**.

Table 2.3. Place Value Chart

1,000,000	100,000	10,000	1,000	100	10	1		$\frac{1}{10}$	$\frac{1}{100}$
10^6	10^5	10^4	10^3	10^2	10^1	10^0	.	10^{-1}	10^{-2}
millions	hundred thousands	ten thousands	thousands	hundreds	tens	ones	decimal	tenths	hundredths

To **add decimal numbers**, line up digits with the same place value. This can be accomplished by writing the numbers vertically and lining up the decimal points. Add zeros as needed so that all the numbers have the same number of decimal places.

To **subtract decimal numbers**, follow the same procedure: write the numbers vertically, lining up the decimal points and adding zeros as necessary.

It is not necessary to line up decimal points to multiply decimal numbers. Simply multiply the numbers, ignoring the decimal point. Then, add together the total number of decimal places in the factors. The product should have the same number of decimal places as this total.

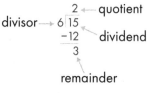

To **divide decimal numbers**, write the problem in long division format. Move the decimal point in the divisor all the way to the right, so that the divisor is a whole number. Move the decimal point in the dividend the same number of places. Position the decimal point in the quotient directly above its new place in the dividend. Then divide, ignoring the decimal point. If necessary, add zeros to the dividend until there is no remainder.

Figure 2.4. Division Terms

PRACTICE QUESTIONS

1. A customer at a restaurant ordered a drink that cost $2.20, a meal that cost $32.54, and a dessert that cost $4. How much was the total bill?

Answer:

Rewrite the numbers vertically, lining up the decimal point.

```
  2.20
 32.54
+ 4.00
 38.74
```

The meal cost **$38.74**.

2. A carnival ride rotates 2.15 times per minute. If a rider is on the ride for 3.5 minutes, how many times did the rider rotate?

Answer:

This is a multiplication problem.

$2.15 \times 3.5 =$

First, multiply the factors, ignoring the decimal point.

$215 \times 35 = 7525$

The factors have a total of three decimal places, so the answer is **7.525 rotations**.

3. $1.324 \div 0.05 =$

Answer:

The decimal point in the divisor needs to be moved two places to the right, so move it two places to the right in the divisor as well. Then position the decimal point in the quotient.

```
           26.48
  005 | 132.40
      - 10
        32
      - 30
         24
       - 20
          40
        - 40
           0
```

Converting Fractions and Decimals

To convert a decimal number to a fraction, write the digits in the numerator and write the place value of the final digit in the denominator. Reduce to lowest terms, if necessary.

To convert a fraction to a decimal, divide the numerator by the denominator.

PRACTICE QUESTIONS

1. Convert 0.096 to a fraction.

Answer:

The final digit is in the thousandths place, so 0.096 is $\frac{96}{1000}$.

Simplify the fraction by dividing the numerator and the denominator by their greatest common factor.

$$\frac{96 \div 8}{1000 \div 8} = \frac{12}{125}$$

2. Convert $\frac{5}{8}$ to a decimal.

Answer:

```
      0.625
  8│5.000
   − 48
      20
    − 16
      40
    − 40
       0
```

Ratios

A **ratio** is a comparison of two quantities. For example, if a class consists of fifteen women and ten men, the ratio of women to men is 15 to 10. This ratio can also be written as 15:10 or $\frac{15}{10}$. Ratios, like fractions, can be reduced by dividing by common factors.

PRACTICE QUESTION

A company employs 30 people, 12 of whom are men. What is the ratio of women to men working at the company?

Answer:

Find the number of women working at the company.

30 − 12 = 18 women

Write the ratio as the number of women over the number of men working at the company.

$$\frac{\text{number of women}}{\text{number of men}} = \frac{18}{12}$$

Reduce the ratio.

$$\frac{18 \div 6}{12 \div 6} = \frac{3}{2}$$

The ratio of women to men is $\frac{3}{2}$ or **3:2**.

Proportions

A **proportion** is a statement that two ratios are equal. For example, proportion $\frac{5}{10} = \frac{7}{14}$ is true because both ratios are equal to $\frac{1}{2}$.

The cross product is found by multiplying the top of one fraction by the bottom of the other (*across* the equal sign).

Cross product: $\frac{a}{b} = \frac{c}{d} \rightarrow ad = bc$

Proportions have a useful quality: their cross products are equal.

$$\frac{5}{10} = \frac{7}{14}$$

$$5(14) = 7(10)$$

$$70 = 70$$

The fact that the cross products of proportions are equal can be used to solve proportions in which one of the values is missing. Use x to stand in for the missing variable, then cross multiply and solve.

PRACTICE QUESTION

The dosage for a particular medication is proportional to the weight of the patient. If the dosage for a patient weighing 60 kg is 90 mg, what is the dosage for a patient weighing 80 kg?

Answer:

Write a proportion using x for the missing value.

$$\frac{60 \text{ kg}}{90 \text{ mg}} = \frac{80 \text{ kg}}{x \text{ mg}}$$

Cross multiply.

$$60(x) = 80(90)$$

$$60x = 7200$$

Divide by 60.

$$x = 120$$

The proper dosage is **120 mg**.

Percents

A **percent** (or percentage) means *per hundred* and is expressed with the percent symbol, %. For example, 54% means 54 out of every 100. Percents are turned into decimals by moving the decimal point two places to the left, so 54% = 0.54. Percentages can be solved by setting up a proportion:

$$\frac{\text{part}}{\text{whole}} = \frac{\%}{100}$$

PRACTICE QUESTION

On one day, a radiology clinic had 80% of patients come in for their scheduled appointments. If they saw 16 patients, how many scheduled appointments did the clinic have that week?

Answer:

Set up a proportion and solve.

$$\frac{part}{whole} = \frac{\%}{100}$$

$$\frac{16}{x} = \frac{80}{100}$$

$$16(100) = 80(x)$$

$$x = 20$$

There were **20 scheduled appointments** that day.

Estimation and Rounding

Estimation is the process of rounding numbers before performing operations in order to make those operations easier. Estimation can be used when an exact answer is not necessary or to check work.

To round a number, first identify the digit in the specified place. Then look at the digit one place to the right. If that digit is 4 or less, keep the digit in the specified place the same. If that digit is 5 or more, add 1 to the digit in the specified place. All the digits to the right of the specified place become zeros.

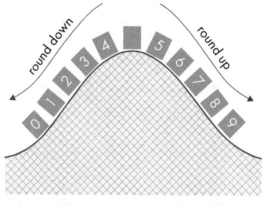

Figure 2.5. Rounding

PRACTICE QUESTION

In September, Alicia's electric bill was $49.22, and her water bill was $22.14. Estimate the total of her utilities for September.

Answer:

Solve the problem by rounding the expenses to the nearest $10.

$49.22 rounds up to $50 because the digit in the ones place is 9.

$22.14 rounds down to $20 because the digit in the ones place is 2.

50 + 20 = 70, so Alicia's September utilities are about **$70**.

Statistics

A **measure of central tendency** is a single value used to describe or represent a set of data. Three common measures of central tendency are mean, median, and mode. A **measure of spread** is a value used to describe the dispersion of data. The simplest measure of spread is range.

A **mean** is an average. The mean is computed by adding all the data and dividing by the number of data points.

The **median** of a set of data is the middle number when the data is ranked (put in order). A data set with an even number of data points will have two numbers in the middle. When that is the case, the median is the mean of those two numbers.

The **range** of a set of data is the difference between the greatest and the least values in the set.

PRACTICE QUESTION

Zoe has 6 tests in her chemistry class. Her scores were 75, 62, 78, 92, 83, and 90. What are the mean, median, and range of her test scores?

Answer:

To find the mean, add her scores and divide by 6:

75 + 62 + 78 + 92 + 83 + 90 = 480

$\frac{480}{6}$ = **80**

To find the median, put the scores in order and find the middle term:

From smallest to largest, the data is 62, 75, 78, 83, 90, 92.

The two middle numbers are 78 and 83.

$\frac{78 + 83}{2}$ = **80.5**

To find the range of Zoe's test scores, subtract the lowest score from the highest score:

92 − 62 = **30**

Units

The United States uses customary units, sometimes called **standard units.** In this system, there are a number of different units that can be used to describe the same variable. These units and the relationships between them are shown in Table 2.4.

Table 2.4. US Customary Units

Variable Measured	Unit	Conversions
Length	inches, foot, yard, mile	12 inches = 1 foot 3 feet = 1 yard 5,280 feet = 1 mile
Weight	ounces, pound, ton	16 ounces = 1 pound 2,000 pounds = 1 ton
Volume	fluid ounces, cup, pint, quart, gallon	8 fluid ounces = 1 cup 2 cups = 1 pint 2 pints = 1 quart 4 quarts = 1 gallon
Time	second, minute, hour, day	60 seconds = 1 minute 60 minutes = 1 hour 24 hours = 1 day
Area	square inch, square foot, square yard	144 square inches = 1 square foot 9 square feet = 1 square yard

Most other countries use the metric system, which has its own set of units for variables like length, weight, and volume. These units are modified by prefixes that make large and small numbers easier to handle. These units and prefixes are shown in Table 2.5.

Table 2.5. Metric Units and Prefixes

Variable Measured	Base Unit
length	meter
weight	gram
volume	liter

Metric Prefix	Conversion
kilo	base unit × 1,000
hecto	base unit × 100
deka	base unit × 10
deci	base unit × 0.1
centi	base unit × 0.01
milli	base unit × 0.001

Conversion factors are used to convert one unit to another (either within the same system or between different systems). A conversion factor is simply a fraction built from two equivalent values. For example, there are 12 inches in 1 foot, so the conversion factor can be $\frac{12\,\text{in}}{1\,\text{ft}}$ or $\frac{1\,\text{ft}}{12\,\text{in}}$.

To convert from one unit to another, multiple the original value by a conversion factor that has the old and new units.

How many inches are in 6 feet?

$$6\,\text{ft} \times \frac{12\,\text{in}}{1\,\text{ft}} = \frac{6\,\text{ft} \times 12\,\text{in}}{1\,\text{ft}} = 72\,\text{in}$$

PRACTICE QUESTIONS

1. How many centimeters are in 2.5 m?

   Answer:

   Use a conversion factor to convert centimeters to meters.

   $$2.5\,\text{m} \times \frac{100\,\text{cm}}{1\,\text{m}} = \frac{2.5\,\text{m} \times 100\,\text{cm}}{1\,\text{m}} = \mathbf{250\,cm}$$

2. A newborn baby will consume 4 ounces of milk per meal and eats 6 times a day. If the baby's mother is storing the milk in pints, how many pints will she need in a week?

   Answer:

   Find the total number of ounces the baby will consume in a week.

   4 oz × 6 meals a day × 7 days = 168 oz

   Use a conversion factor to convert ounces to pints.

   $$168\,\text{oz} \times \frac{1\,\text{cu}}{8\,\text{oz}} \times \frac{1\,\text{pt}}{2\,\text{cu}} = \mathbf{10.5\,pt}$$

Test Your Knowledge

Work the problem, and then choose the correct answer.

1. 65 − 14.46 + 5.8 =

    a. 14.53   b. 15.69   c. 44.74   d. 56.34   e. 73.66

2. 4.368 ÷ 2.8 =

    a. 0.0156   b. 0.156   c. 1.56   d. 15.6   e. 156

3. Find the product of 0.4 and 0.2.

    a. 0.006   b. 0.06   c. 0.08   d. 0.6   e. 0.8

4. Noah and Jennifer have a total of $10.00 to spend on lunch. If each buys his or her own order of french fries and a soda, how many orders of chicken strips can they share?

Menu	
Item	**Price**
Hamburger	$4.00
Chicken Strips	$4.00
Onion Rings	$3.00
French Fries	$2.00
Soda	$1.00
Shake	$1.00

    a. 0   b. 1   c. 2   d. 3   e. 4

5. A fruit stand sells apples, bananas, and oranges at a ratio of 3:2:1. If the fruit stand sells 20 bananas, how many total pieces of fruit does the fruit stand sell?

    a. 10   b. 30   c. 40   d. 50   e. 60

6. Juan plans to spend 25% of his workday writing a report. If he is at work for 9 hours, how many hours will he spend writing the report?

    a. 2.25   b. 2.50   c. 2.75   d. 3.25   e. 4.00

7. John's rain gauge recorded rain on three consecutive days: $\frac{1}{2}$ in on Sunday, $\frac{2}{3}$ in on Monday, and $\frac{1}{4}$ in on Tuesday. What was the total amount of rain received over the three days?

    a. $\frac{4}{9}$ in   b. $\frac{17}{36}$ in   c. $1\frac{5}{12}$ in   d. $1\frac{1}{2}$ in   e. $1\frac{2}{3}$ in

8. A woman's dinner bill is $48.30. If she adds a 20% tip, what will she pay in total?

a. $9.66   b. $28.98   c. $38.64   d. $57.96   e. $68.30

9. Frank and Josh need 1 lb of chocolate to bake a cake. If Frank has $\frac{3}{8}$ lb of chocolate, and Josh has $\frac{1}{2}$ lb, how much more chocolate do they need?

a. $\frac{1}{10}$ lb   b. $\frac{1}{8}$ lb   c. $\frac{3}{5}$ lb   d. $\frac{7}{8}$ lb   e. $\frac{9}{10}$ lb

10. Students in a biology class get the following scores on a test:

97, 83, 81, 70, 64, 92, 87

What was the average score?

a. 64   b. 71   c. 82   d. 92   e. 96

1. d.

Line up the decimals and subtract.

$$\begin{array}{r} 65.00 \\ -\ 14.46 \\ \hline 50.54 \end{array}$$

Line up the decimals and add.

$$\begin{array}{r} 50.54 \\ +\ 5.80 \\ \hline \mathbf{56.34} \end{array}$$

2. c.

$4.368 \div 2.8 = \mathbf{1.56}$

3. c.

$0.4 \times 0.2 = \mathbf{0.08}$

4. b.

Write an expression to find the number of chicken strips they can afford:

$\$10 - 2(\$2.00 + \$1.00)$

$= \$10 - 2(\$3.00)$

$= \$10 - \$6.00 = \$4.00$

Four dollars is enough money to buy **one order** of chicken strips to share.

5. e.

Assign variables and write the ratios as fractions. Then, cross multiply to solve for the number of apples and oranges sold.

$\dfrac{apples}{bananas} = \dfrac{3}{2} = \dfrac{x}{20}$

$60 = 2x$

$x = 30$ apples

$\dfrac{oranges}{bananas} = \dfrac{1}{2} = \dfrac{y}{20}$

$2y = 20$

$y = 10$ oranges

To find the total, add the number of apples, oranges, and bananas together.

$30 + 20 + 10 = \mathbf{60\ pieces\ of\ fruit}$

6. a.

Use the equation for percentages.

part = whole × percentage = $9 \times 0.25 = \mathbf{2.25}$

7. c.

$\dfrac{1}{2} + \dfrac{2}{3} + \dfrac{1}{4}$

$\dfrac{6}{12} + \dfrac{8}{12} + \dfrac{3}{12} = \dfrac{17}{12} = \mathbf{1\dfrac{5}{12}}$ **in**

8. d.

Multiply the total bill by 0.2 (20%) to find the amount of the tip. Then add the tip to the total.

$\$48.30 \times 0.2 = \$9.66$

$\$48.30 + \$9.66 = \mathbf{\$57.96}$

9. b.

$\dfrac{3}{8} + \dfrac{1}{2} = \dfrac{3}{8} + \dfrac{4}{8} = \dfrac{7}{8}$

$1 - \dfrac{7}{8} = \dfrac{8}{8} - \dfrac{7}{8} = \mathbf{\dfrac{1}{8}}$ **lb**

10. c.

Add the scores and divide by 7:

$\dfrac{97 + 83 + 81 + 70 + 64 + 92 + 87}{7} = \dfrac{574}{7} = \mathbf{82}$

THREE: NONVERBAL SUBTEST

The twenty-five nonverbal questions on the Academic Aptitude test will gauge your spatial visualization and reasoning skills. You will be shown an analogy built from basic shapes, and you will need to select from the five answer choices to complete the analogy.

> **Nonverbal Question Format**
>
> Which shape correctly completes the statement?
>
> ◯ is to ○ as ▢ is to **?**
>
> a.○ b.▢ c.△ d.▢ e.◇

What is an Analogy?

An **analogy** presents two sets of words or objects that share a relationship. The relationship is set up using the format

> _____ is to _____ as _____ is to _____

Let's start with an example that uses words instead of shapes.

> BIRD is to FLOCK as WOLF is to PACK

In this analogy, the first word is an individual animal, and the second word represents a group of those animals. A group of birds is a flock, and a group of wolves is a pack.

Solving analogies requires you to determine the relationship between the first two words, and then use that relationship to fill in the missing word:

> SAIL is to BOAT as FLY is to_____

Here, the missing word is *plane*: you sail on a boat and fly on a plane.

Nonverbal Analogies

The nonverbal questions on the test will be in this same format, but they will use shapes instead of words. To answer these questions, you should look for the common relationships between the first two shapes.

ROTATING SHAPES

The first shape is rotated 90 degrees clockwise to give the second shape. To find the missing shape, rotate the cube 90 degrees clockwise as well.

ADDING TO SHAPES

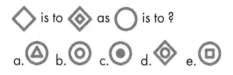

To create the second shape, another diamond is added inside the first. To find the missing shape, add another circle inside the first one.

SUBTRACTING FROM SHAPES

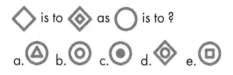

The bottom diamond is removed from the first shape to create the second. To find the missing shape, remove the bottom circle.

COMBINATIONS

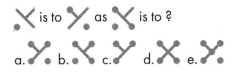

In this question, the first shape is reflected horizontally (as if shown in a mirror). Then, another circle is added to the end of the top line. To find the missing shape, reflect the given shape and add a circle to the end of the top line.

Test Your Knowledge

Which shape correctly completes the statement?

1. ⊖ is to ◑ as ⊖ is to ?

   a. ● b. ◑ c. ⊖ d. ◐ e. ○

2. △ is to ☐ as ⬠ is to ?

   a. ◺ b. ▭ c. ⬡ d. ○ e. ◇

3. | is to ┬ as ╫ is to ?

   a. ╪ b. ≣ c. ☐ d. ╫ e. ╫

4. ⬠ is to ◇ as ◁ is to ?

   a. △ b. ▭ c. ◺ d. ◁ e. ▽

5. ❖ is to ❖ as ❖ is to ?

   a. ⬙ b. ❖ c. ❖ d. ❖ e. ❖

6. ⊪ is to ⊪ as ⊪ is to ?

   a. ⊪ b. ⊪ c. ⊪ d. ⊪ e. ⊪

7. ◱ is to ◱ as ◳ is to ?

   a. ◱ b. ◱ c. ◱ d. ◳ e. ◱

8. ⦂ is to ⦂ as ⦂ is to ?

   a. ⦂ b. ⦂ c. ⦂ d. ⦂ e. ⦂

9. ⌐ is to | as ⊔ is to ?

   a. ⌐ b. ⊏ c. || d. ⊐ e. ⊓

10. ⊏ is to ⊐ as ⊐ is to ?

    a. ⊐ b. ⊏ c. ⊐ d. ⊐ e. ⊏

ANSWER KEY

1. d.

Rotate the first shape 90 degrees clockwise to create the second shape.

2. c.

Add one side to the first shape to create the second shape.

3. d.

Add a horizontal line to the first shape to create the second shape.

4. d.

Cut the first shape in half horizontally to create the second shape.

5. c.

Change the right diamond to a circle in the first shape to create the second shape.

6. b.

Shorten the inside lines of the first shape to create the second shape.

7. b.

The second shape is a horizontal reflection of the first shape.

8. d.

Add a circle to the side that has one circle on the first shape to create the second shape.

9. c.

Remove the bottom bar from the first shape to create the second shape.

10. a.

Reflect the first shape vertically and reverse the shading to create the second shape.

FOUR: SPELLING

The forty-five spelling questions will test your ability to pick out the correct spelling of a word from a list of three choices.

> **Spelling Question Format**
>
> *Each line below contains a word with three different spellings. Select the word from each line that is spelled correctly.*
>
> **1.** a. intense b. intinse c. entense

As with the verbal questions, a large vocabulary will help you on this section. But when you encounter words you're not familiar with, it will help to know some basic spelling rules. You can also study the list of commonly misspelled words included at the end of this chapter.

Spelling Rule One: Plurals

Regular nouns are made plural by adding *s*. Irregular nouns can follow many different rules for pluralization, which are summarized in Table 4.1.

Table 4.1. Irregular Plural Nouns

Ends with...	Make it plural by...	Example
y	changing *y* to *i* and adding –*es*	baby → babies
f	changing *f* to *v* and adding –*es*	leaf → leaves
fe	changing *f* to *v* and adding –*s*	knife → knives
us	changing *us* to *i*	nucleus → nuclei

Table 4.1. Irregular Plural Nouns (continued)

Ends with...	Make it plural by...	Example
ch, o, s, sh, x, z	adding –es	catch → catches potato → potatoes pass → passes push → pushes annex → annexes blitz → blitzes

Always the same	Doesn't follow the rules
sheep	man → men
deer	child → children
fish	person → people
moose	tooth → teeth
pants	goose → geese
binoculars	mouse → mice
scissors	ox → oxen

Spelling Rule Two: Conjugating Verbs

The suffixes –ed or –ing added to a regular verb generally signify the verb's tense. However, there are some exceptions to the general rule for conjugating regular verbs.

When verbs end with a silent –e, drop the e before adding –ed or –ing.

fake → faked → faking

ache → ached → aching

When verbs end in the letters –ee, do not drop the second e. Instead, simply add –d or –ing.

free → freed → freeing

agree → agreed → agreeing

When the verb ends with a single vowel plus a consonant, and the stress is at the end of the word, then the consonant must be doubled before adding –ed or –ing.

commit → committed → committing

refer → referred → referring

If the stress is not at the end of the word, then the consonant can remain singular.

target → targeted → targeting

visit → visited → visiting

Verbs that end with the letter –c must have the letter k added before receiving a suffix.

panic → panicked → panicking

Spelling Rule Three: i before e

Generally, the letter i comes before the letter e in a word except when the i is preceded by the letter c.

piece

salient

ceiling

conceivable

There are some notable exceptions where the letter e comes before the letter i such as:

+ words that end in –cien, like proficient
+ plural words ending in –cies, like policies
+ words with an ay sound, like eight, vein, or neighbor

 Helpful Hint: Be cautious of the rule "i comes before e except after c" because it has many exceptions. Your foreign neighbors weighed the iciest beige glaciers!

Spelling Rule Four: Suffixes

Change the final –y to an i when adding a suffix.

lazy → laziest

tidy → tidily

For words that end with the letters –le, replace the letter e with the letter y.

subtle → subtly

Commonly Misspelled Words

Table 4.2 shows some commonly misspelled words. It outlines the word as correctly spelled, followed by tips to ensure proper spelling.

Table 4.2. Commonly Misspelled Words

Correct Spelling	Tip
acceptable	has two c's and remember, you are *able* to accept
accommodate, accommodation	double up the *c* and *m*
acquire, acquit	add a *c* before *qu*
aggressive, aggression	spelled with two g's
apparently	*ent*, not *ant*
appearance	ends with −*ance*, not −*ence*
assassination	two sets of double *s*, like Mississippi
basically	ends with −*ally*
beginning	add an *n* before adding the −*ing*
bizarre	spelled with one *z* and two *r*'s
calendar	ends with −*ar*, not −*er*
colleague	The second half is *league*, as in baseball; colleagues are like teammates!
completely	do not drop the *e*; ends with −*ely*
conscious	spelled with an *s* and *c* in the middle
definitely	spelled with *ite*, not *ate*
dilemma	double *m*
disappear	spelled with one *s* and two *p's*
disappoint	spelled with one *s* and two *p's*
discipline	spelled with an *s* and *c* in the middle; *i* instead of *a*
embarrass	double up *r* and *s*
environment	an *n* comes before the *m*
existence	ends with −*ence*
finally	spelled with two *l's*
fluorescent	begins with *fluor*− and ends with −*scent*
foreign	*e* before *i*, an exception to the *ie* rule
foreseeable	begins with *fore*−, not *for*−
forty	begins with *for*−, not *four*−
forward	begins with *for*−, not *fo*−
further	begins with *fur*−, not *fu*−
gist	begins with *g*, not *j*
government	there is an *n* before the *m*
harass, harassment	spelled with one *r*, and two *s's*

Correct Spelling	Tip
idiosyncrasy	ends with –asy, not –acy
incidentally	ends with –ally
independent	ends with –ent, not –ant
interrupt	spelled with two r's
irresistible	ends with –ible
knowledge	remember the silent d
liaise, liaison	there is an i before and after the a: iai
necessary	spelled with one c and two s's
noticeable	do not drop the e when adding –able
occasion	spelled with two c's and one s
occurred, occurring	spelled with two c's and two r's
occurrence	spelled with two c's and two r's, and ends with –ence, not –ance
persistent	ends with –ent, not –ant
possession	two sets of double s like Mississippi
preferred, preferring	the second r is doubled
publicly	simply add –ly to the end of public
recommend	spelled with two m's
reference	ends with –ence, not –ance
referred, referring	the second r is doubled
relevant	ends with –ant, not –ent
resistance	ends with –ance
sense	ends with –se
separate	spelled with par in the middle
siege	i before e rule
successful	double up the c's and s's
supersede	ends with –sede
surprise	begins with sur–, not su–
tendency	ends with –ency, not –ancy
tomorrow	spelled with one m and two r's
tongue	begins with ton– and ends with –gue
unforeseen	spelled with an e after the r
unfortunately	do not drop the e when adding –ly
until	spelled with one l at the end
weird	e before i, an exception to the rule

Test Your Knowledge

Each line below contains a word with three different spellings. Select the word from each line that is spelled correctly.

1.	a. supervise	b. supervice	c. supirvise
2.	a. casuelty	b. casualty	c. cacualtie
3.	a. intensity	b. entensity	c. intensitie
4.	a. acelerate	b. accelarate	c. accelerate
5.	a. permenent	b. permanent	c. permanant
6.	a. abundent	b. abbundant	c. abundant
7.	a. burdan	b. burden	c. bourden
8.	a. prioritys	b. priorities	c. prioretees
9.	a. immense	b. emmense	c. emmence
10.	a. contaminate	b. contamenate	c. conntaminate
11.	a. arterys	b. arteries	c. artarys
12.	a. nutrishon	b. nutrition	c. nutretion
13.	a. accomplesh	b. acommplish	c. accomplish
14.	a. comppasion	b. compassion	c. commpasion
15.	a. courteous	b. corteous	c. curtaous

CONTINUE

ANSWER KEY

1. a.
2. b.
3. a.
4. c.
5. b.
6. c.
7. b.
8. b.

9. a.
10. a.
11. b.
12. b.
13. c.
14. b.
15. a.

FIVE: READING

The thirty-five reading questions will test your ability to understand the purpose, structure, and key ideas of written passages. The test will present short passages, often on a scientific topic, that are followed by a set of questions with four answer choices.

> **Reading Question Format**
>
> *Read each passage carefully. Each question is followed by four suggested answers. You are to decide which one of these answers you should choose based upon the material in the passage.*
>
> In 1953, doctors surgically removed the hippocampus of patient Henry Molaison in an attempt to stop his frequent seizures. Unexpectedly, he lost the ability to form new memories, leading to the biggest breakthrough in the science of memory. Molaison's long-term memory—of events more than a year before his surgery—was unchanged as was his ability to learn physical skills.
>
> **1.** After surgery to remove his hippocampus, Henry Molaison no longer
>
> a. formed new memories b. had seizures c. learned physical skills
> d. remembered his past

The Main Idea

The **topic** is a word or short phrase that explains what a passage is about. The **main idea** is a complete sentence that explains what the author is trying to say about the topic. Generally, the **topic sentence** is the first (or near the first) sentence in a paragraph. It is a general statement that introduces the topic so that the reader knows what to expect.

 Check Your Understanding: To find the main idea, identify the topic and then ask, *What is the author trying to tell me about the topic?*

The **summary sentence**, on the other hand, frequently (but not always!) comes at the end of a paragraph or passage because it wraps up all the ideas presented. This sentence summarizes what an author has said about the topic. Some passages, particularly short ones, will not include a summary sentence.

Table 5.1. Identifying Topic and Main Idea	
The cisco, a foot-long freshwater fish native to the Great Lakes, once thrived throughout the basin but had virtually disappeared by the 1950s. However, today fishermen are pulling them up by the net load in Lake Michigan and Lake Ontario. It is highly unusual for a native species to revive, and the reason for the cisco's reemergence is even more unlikely. The cisco have an invasive species—quagga mussels—to thank for their return. Quagga mussels depleted nutrients in the lakes, harming other species highly dependent on these nutrients. Cisco, however, thrive in low-nutrient environments. As other species—many of which were invasive—diminished, cisco flourished in their place.	
topic sentence	The cisco, a foot-long freshwater fish native to the Great Lakes, once thrived throughout the basin but had virtually disappeared by the 1950s.
topic	cisco
summary sentence	As other species—many of which were invasive—diminished, cisco flourished in their place.
main idea	Cisco had nearly disappeared from the lake but now flourish thanks to the invasive quagga mussels.

PRACTICE QUESTIONS

Tourists flock to Yellowstone National Park each year to view the geysers that bubble and erupt throughout it. What most of these tourists do not know is that these geysers are formed by a caldera—a hot crater in the earth's crust—which was created by a series of three eruptions of an ancient super volcano. These eruptions, which began 2.1 million years ago, spewed between 1,000 and 2,450 cubic kilometers of volcanic matter at such a rate that the volcano's magma chamber collapsed, creating the craters.

1. This paragraph is chiefly concerned with

    a. tourists b. geysers c. volcanic eruptions d. super volcanos

    Answer:

    b. The topic of the passage is geysers. Tourists, volcanic eruptions, and super volcanos are all mentioned in the explanation of what geysers are and how they are formed.

The Battle of Little Bighorn, commonly called Custer's Last Stand, was a battle between the Lakota, the Northern Cheyenne, the Arapaho, and the Seventh Cavalry Regiment of the US Army. Led by war leaders Crazy Horse and Chief Gall and the religious leader Sitting Bull, the allied tribes of the Plains Indians decisively defeated their US foes. Two hundred and sixty-eight US soldiers were killed, including General George Armstrong Custer, two of his brothers, his nephew, his brother-in-law, and six Indian scouts.

2. The main idea of the passage is that

    a.   most of General Custer's family died in the Battle of Little Bighorn

    b.   the Seventh Cavalry regiment was formed to fight Native American tribes

    c.   Sitting Bull and George Custer were fierce enemies

    d.   the Battle of Little Bighorn was a significant victory for the Plains Indians

<u>Answer:</u>

d. The author writes that "the allied tribes...decisively defeated their US foes," and the remainder of the passage provides details to support this idea.

Supporting Details

Statements that describe or explain the main idea are **supporting details**. Supporting details are often found after the topic sentence. They support the main idea through examples, descriptions, and explanations.

 Helpful Hint: To find supporting details, look for sentences that connect to the main idea and tell more about it.

Authors may add details to support their argument or claim. **Facts** are details that point to truths, while **opinions** are based on personal beliefs or judgments. To differentiate between fact and opinion, look for statements that express feelings, attitudes, or beliefs that can't be proven (opinions) and statements that can be proven (facts).

Table 5.2. Supporting Details and Fact and Opinion

Bait is an important element of fishing. Some people use live bait, such as worms and night crawlers. Others use artificial bait, such as lures and spinners. Live bait has a scent that fish are drawn to. Live bait is a good choice for fishing. It's cheap and easy to find. Lures can vibrate, make noise, and mimic the movements of some fish. People should choose artificial bait over live bait because it can be used multiple times.

supporting details	Lures can vibrate, make noise, and mimic the movements of some fish.
fact	Live bait has a scent that fish are drawn to.
opinion	Live bait is a good choice for fishing.

PRACTICE QUESTIONS

The greatest changes in sensory, motor, and perceptual development happen in the first two years of life. When babies are first born, most of their senses operate in a similar way to those of adults. For example, babies are able to hear before they are born; studies show that babies turn toward the sound of their mothers' voices just minutes after being born, indicating they recognize the mother's voice from their time in the womb.

The exception to this rule is vision. A baby's vision changes significantly in his or her first year of life; initially babies have a range of vision of only 8 – 12 inches and no depth perception. As a result, infants rely primarily on hearing; vision does not become the dominant sense until around the age of 12 months.

1. To perceive the world, babies primarily rely on

    a. vision b. hearing c. touch d. smell

    Answer:

    b.   The passage states that "infants rely primarily on hearing."

2. In the first year of life, a baby has no

    a. depth perception b. vision c. hearing d. motor skills

    Answer:

    a.   The passage states that "[a] baby's vision changes significantly in its first year of life; initially babies have a range of vision of only 8 – 12 inches and no depth perception."

Drawing Conclusions

Readers can use information that is **explicit**, or clearly stated, along with information that is **implicit**, or indirect, to make inferences and **draw conclusions**. Readers can determine meaning from what is implied by using details, context clues, and prior knowledge. When answering questions, consider what is known from personal experiences and make note of all information the author has provided before drawing a conclusion.

> Helpful Hint: Look for facts, character actions and dialogue, how each sentence connects to the topic, and the author's reasoning for an argument when drawing conclusions.

Table 5.3. Drawing Conclusions

When the Spanish-American War broke out in 1898, the US Army was small and under-staffed. President William McKinley called for 1,250 volunteers to serve in the First US Volunteer Cavalry. The ranks were quickly filled by cowboys, gold prospectors, hunters, gamblers, Native Americans, veterans, police officers, and college students looking for an adventure. The officer corps was composed of veterans of previous wars. With more volunteers than it could accept, the army set high standards: all the recruits had to be skilled on horseback and with guns. Consequently, they became known as the Rough Riders.

question	Why are the volunteers named Rough Riders?
explicit information	different people volunteered, men were looking for adventure, recruits had to be extremely skilled on horseback and with guns due to a glut of volunteers
implicit information	Men had previous occupations; officer corps veterans worked with volunteers.
conclusion drawn	The men were called Rough Riders because they were inexperienced yet particularly enthusiastic to help with the war and were willing to put in extra effort to join.

PRACTICE QUESTION

Alfie closed his eyes and took several deep breaths. He was trying to ignore the sounds of the crowd, but even he had to admit it was hard not to notice the tension in the stadium. He could feel 50,000 sets of eyes burning through his skin—this crowd expected perfection from him. He took another breath and opened his eyes, setting his sights on the soccer ball resting peacefully in the grass. One shot, just one last shot, between his team and the championship. He didn't look up at the goalie, who was jumping nervously on the goal line just a few yards away. Afterward, Alfie would swear he didn't remember anything between the referee's whistle and the thunderous roar of the crowd.

At the end of the passage, it's most likely that Alfie

a.   passed out on the field and was unable to take the shot

b.   had his shot blocked by the goalie

c.   scored the goal and won his team the championship

d.   was too scared to take the shot

Answer:

c.   The crowd's support for Alfie and their collective roar after the shot imply that Alfie scored the goal and won the championship.

The Author's Purpose and Point of View

The **author's purpose** is an author's reason for writing a text. Authors may write to share an experience, entertain, persuade, or inform readers. This can be done through persuasive, expository, and narrative writing.

Persuasive writing influences the actions and thoughts of readers. Authors state an opinion, and then provide reasons that support the opinion. **Expository writing** outlines and explains steps in a process. Authors focus on a sequence of events. **Narrative**

writing tells a story. Authors include a setting, plot, characters, problem, and solution in the text.

> ✎ Study Tip: Use the acronym **PIES**—*persuade, inform, entertain, state*—to help you remember elements of an author's purpose.

Authors also share their **point of view** (perspectives, attitudes, and beliefs) with readers. Readers can identify the author's point of view by word choice, details, descriptions, and characters' actions. The author's attitude or **tone** can be found in word choice that conveys feelings or stance on a topic.

Text structure is the way the author organizes a text. A text can be organized to show problem and solution, comparison and contrast, or even cause and effect. Structure of a text can give insight into an author's purpose and point of view. If a text is organized to pose an argument or advertise a product, it can be considered persuasive. The author's point of view will be revealed in how thoughts and opinions are expressed in the text.

Table 5.4. The Author's Purpose and Point of View

Superfoods are foods found in nature. They contain rich nutrients and are low in calories. Many people are concerned about healthy diets and weight loss, so superfoods are a great meal choice! Rich antioxidants and vitamins found in superfoods decrease the risk of diseases and aid in heart health.

author's purpose	persuade readers of the benefit of superfoods
point of view	advocate superfoods as "a great meal choice"
tone	positive, encouraging, pointing out the benefits of superfoods, using positive words like *great* and *rich*
structure	cause and effect to show use of superfoods and results

PRACTICE QUESTIONS

University of California, Berkeley, researchers decided to tackle an age-old problem: why shoelaces come untied. They recorded the shoelaces of a volunteer walking on a treadmill by attaching devices to record the acceleration, or g-force, experienced by the knot. The results were surprising. A shoelace knot experiences more g-force from a person walking than any rollercoaster can generate. However, if the person simply stomped or swung his or her feet—the two movements that make up a walker's stride—the g-force was not enough to undo the knots.

1. The purpose of the passage is to

    a. confirm if shoelaces always come undone

    b. compare the force of treadmills and rollercoasters

    c. persuade readers to tie their shoes tighter

    d. describe the results of an experiment on shoelaces

Answer:

d. The text provides details on the experiment as well as its results.

What do you do with plastic bottles? Do you throw them away, or do you recycle or reuse them? As landfills continue to fill up, there will eventually be no place to put our trash. If you recycle or reuse bottles, you will help reduce waste and turn something old into a creative masterpiece!

2. The author of the passage believes that

    a. landfills are unnecessary

    b. reusing objects requires creativity

    c. recycling helps the environment

    d. reusing objects is better than recycling

Answer:

c. The author states that recycling and reusing objects reduce waste, which helps the environment.

Negative cinematic representations of gorillas have provoked fear and contribute to hunting practices that endanger gorilla populations. It's a shame that many films portray them as scary and aggressive creatures. Their size and features should not be cause for alarm. Gorillas are actually shy and act aggressively only when provoked.

3. The main emotion expressed by the author toward gorillas is

    a. surprise   b. concern   c. anger   d. fear

Answer:

b. The author is concerned that the scary depiction of gorillas in cinema is harming public perceptions of the animal.

CONTINUE

Test Your Knowledge

Read each passage carefully. Each question is followed by four suggested answers. You are to decide which one of these answers you should choose based upon the material in the passage.

The cisco, a foot-long freshwater fish native to the Great Lakes, once thrived throughout the basin but had virtually disappeared by the 1950s. However, today fishermen are pulling them up by the net load in Lake Michigan and Lake Ontario. It is highly unusual for a native species to revive, and the reason for the cisco's reemergence is even more unlikely. The cisco have an invasive species—quagga mussels—to thank for their return. Quagga mussels depleted nutrients in the lakes, harming other species highly dependent on these nutrients. Cisco, however, thrive in low-nutrient environments. While quagga mussels caused the death of many other native species, cisco flourished in their place.

1. The cisco population has grown in recent years because of

    a.   quagga mussels

    b.   fishing

    c.   a high-nutrient environment

    d.   the availability of more food

2. In the Great Lakes, quagga mussels have

    a.   died out due to overfishing

    b.   been the main source of food for cisco

    c.   struggled to survive in their new environments

    d.   caused the decline of native species

When a fire destroyed San Francisco's American Indian Center in October of 1969, American Indian groups set their sights on the recently closed island prison of Alcatraz as the site of a new Indian cultural center and school. Ignored by the government, an activist group known as Indians of All Tribes sailed to Alcatraz in the early morning hours with eighty-nine men, women, and children. They landed on Alcatraz, claiming it for all the tribes of North America. Their demands were ignored, and so the group continued to occupy the island for the next nineteen months, its numbers swelling up to 600 as others joined. By January of 1970, many of the original protestors had left, and on June 11, 1971, federal marshals forcibly removed the last residents.

3. In October 1969, Alcatraz was occupied by

    a.   San Francisco's American Indian Center

    b.   Indians of All Tribes

    c.   federal marshals

    d.   prisoners

For thirteen years, a spacecraft called *Cassini* was on an exploratory mission to Saturn. The spacecraft was designed not to return but to end its journey by diving into Saturn's atmosphere. This dramatic ending provided scientists with unprecedented information about Saturn's atmosphere and its magnetic and gravitational fields. First, however, *Cassini* passed Saturn's largest moon, Titan, where it recorded data on Titan's curious methane lakes, gathering information about potential seasons on the planet-sized moon. Then it passed through the unexplored region between Saturn itself and its famous rings. Scientists hope to learn how old the rings are and to directly examine the particles that make them up. *Cassini's* mission ended in 2017, but researchers have new questions for future exploration.

4. The scientists who developed *Cassini* want to learn more about Titan's

    a. gravity
    b. rings
    c. lakes
    d. atmosphere

In a remote nature preserve in northeastern Siberia, scientists are attempting to re-create the subarctic grassland ecosystem that flourished there during the last Ice Age. The area today is dominated by forests, but the lead scientists of the project believe the forested terrain was not a natural development. They believe that if they can restore the grassland, they will be able to slow climate change by slowing the thawing of the permafrost that lies beneath the surface. Key to this undertaking is restoring the wildlife to the region, including wild horses, musk oxen, bison, and yak. Most ambitiously, the scientists hope to revive the woolly mammoth species, which was key in trampling the ground and knocking down the trees, helping to keep the land free for grasses to grow.

5. Today, northeastern Siberia is dominated by

    a. forests
    b. grasslands
    c. wild horses
    d. woolly mammoths

The heart works by shifting between two states: systole and diastole. In systole, the cardiac muscles are contracting and moving blood from any given chamber. During diastole, the muscles are relaxing and the chamber is expanding to fill with blood. The systole and diastole are responsible for blood pressure—the pressure in the major arteries. This is the blood pressure that is measured in a regular exam. The two values are systolic and diastolic pressures, respectively. Because it is measured when blood is being pumped into the arteries, systolic blood pressure is always the higher number.

Systolic blood pressure is correlated with negative health outcomes such as stroke and heart failure. For this reason, doctors categorize patients based on their systolic blood pressure. These categories are given in the following table.

Categories	Systolic Range
normal	< 120
prehypertension	120 – 139
hypertension stage 1	140 – 159
hypertension stage 2	160 – 179
hypertensive crisis	> 180

6. A person with a blood pressure of 151/95 be categorized as

   a.   normal

   b.   prehypertension

   c.   hypertension stage 1

   d.   hypertension stage 2

The social and political discourse of America continues to be permeated with idealism. An idealistic viewpoint asserts that the ideals of freedom, equality, justice, and human dignity are the truths that Americans must continue to aspire to. Idealists argue that truth is what should be, not necessarily what is. In general, they work to improve things and to make them as close to ideal as possible.

7. The purpose of the passage is to

   a.   advocate for freedom, equality, justice, and human rights

   b.   explain what an idealist believes in

   c.   explain what's wrong with social and political discourse in America

   d.   persuade readers to believe in certain truths

Alexander Hamilton and James Madison called for the Constitutional Convention to write a constitution as the foundation of a stronger federal government. Madison and other Federalists like John Adams believed in separation of powers, republicanism, and a strong federal government. Despite the separation of powers that would be provided for in the US Constitution, anti-Federalists like Thomas Jefferson called for even more limitations on the power of the federal government.

8. A strong federal government was NOT supported by

   a.   Alexander Hamilton

   b.   James Madison

   c.   John Adams

   d.   Thomas Jefferson

After looking at five houses, Robert and I have decided to buy the one on Forest Road. The first two homes we visited didn't have the space we need—the first had only one bathroom, and the second did not have a guest bedroom. The third house, on Pine Street, had enough space inside but didn't have a big enough yard for our three dogs. The fourth house we looked at, on Rice Avenue, was stunning but well above our price range. The last home, on Forest Road, wasn't in the neighborhood we wanted to live in. However, it had the right amount of space for the right price.

9. The house on Pine Street
    a. did not have enough bedrooms
    b. did not have a big enough yard
    c. was not in the right neighborhood
    d. was too expensive

The study showed that private tutoring is providing a significant advantage to those students who are able to afford it. Researchers looked at the grades of students who had received free tutoring through the school versus those whose parents had paid for private tutors. The study included 2,500 students in three high schools across four grade levels. The study found that students who used private tutoring increased their grade point average (GPA) by 0.7 points. Students who used the school's free tutor service saw an increase in GPA of 0.3 points on average. Students who used both services showed an increase in GPA of 0.5 points. After reviewing the study, the board is recommending that the school restructure its free tutor service to provide a more equitable education for all students.

10. The students with the largest rise in GPA used
    a. no tutoring
    b. free tutoring
    c. private tutoring
    d. free and private tutoring

It could be said that the great battle between the North and South we call the Civil War was a battle for individual identity. The states of the South had their own culture, one based on farming, independence, and the rights of both man and state to determine their own paths. Similarly, the North had forged its own identity as a center of centralized commerce and manufacturing. This clash of lifestyles was bound to create tension, and this tension was bound to lead to war. But people who try to sell you this narrative are wrong. The Civil War was not a battle of cultural identities—it was a battle about slavery. All other explanations for the war are either a direct consequence of the South's desire for wealth at the expense of her fellow man or a fanciful invention to cover up this sad portion of our nation's history. And it cannot be denied that this time in our past was very sad indeed.

11. The purpose of the passage is to
    a. convince readers that slavery was the main cause of the Civil War
    b. illustrate the cultural differences between the North and the South before the Civil War
    c. persuade readers that the North deserved to win the Civil War
    d. demonstrate that the history of the Civil War is too complicated to be understood clearly

12. Before the Civil War, the North had a culture based on

    a.   farming

    b.   independence

    c.   rights of the state

    d.   centralized commerce

The bacteria, fungi, insects, plants, and animals that live together in a habitat have evolved to share a pool of limited resources. They've competed for water, minerals, nutrients, sunlight, and space—sometimes for thousands or even millions of years. As these communities have evolved, the species in them have developed complex, long-term interspecies interactions known as symbiotic relationships.

Ecologists characterize these interactions based on whether each party benefits. In mutualism, both individuals benefit, while in synnecrosis, both organisms are harmed. A relationship where one individual benefits and the other is harmed is known as parasitism. Examples of these relationships can easily be seen in any ecosystem. Pollination, for example, is mutualistic—pollinators get nutrients from the flower, and the plant is able to reproduce—whereas tapeworms, which steal nutrients from their host, are parasitic.

There's yet another class of symbiosis that is <u>controversial</u> among scientists. As it's long been defined, commensalism is a relationship where one species benefits and the other is unaffected. But is it possible for two species to interact and for one to remain completely unaffected? Often, relationships described as commensal include one species that feeds on another species' leftovers; remoras, for instance, will attach themselves to sharks and eat the food particles they leave behind. It might seem like the shark gets nothing from the relationship, but a closer look will show that sharks in fact benefit from remoras, which clean the sharks' skin and remove parasites. In fact, many scientists claim that relationships currently described as commensal are just mutualistic or parasitic in ways that haven't been discovered yet.

13. In the last paragraph, the word *controversial* means

    a.   debatable

    b.   disbelieved

    c.   confusing

    d.   upsetting

14. The relationship between a tapeworm and its host is

    a.   mutualism

    b.   commensalism

    c.   parasitism

    d.   synnecrosis

15. The purpose of the passage is to

    a.   argue that commensalism isn't actually found in nature

    b.   describe the many types of symbiotic relationships

    c.   explain how competition for resources results in long-term interspecies relationships

    d.   provide examples of the many different ways individual organisms interact

ANSWER KEY

1. a.

The passage explains how quagga mussels depleted the nutrients in the lake, allowing cisco to thrive.

2. d.

The author writes that the "quagga mussels caused the death of many other native species."

3. b.

The "Indians of All Tribes sailed to Alcatraz" because they wanted to develop a cultural center and school at the site.

4. c.

The author writes that the *Cassini* "recorded data on Titan's curious methane lakes."

5. a.

The passage states that "[t]he area today is dominated by forests."

6. c.

A systolic blood pressure reading of 151 (the higher number) places the patient in the hypertension stage 1 category.

7. b.

The purpose of the passage is to explain what an idealist believes in. The author does not offer any opinions or try to persuade readers about the importance of certain values.

8. d.

In the passage, Thomas Jefferson is defined as an anti-Federalist, in contrast with Federalists who believed in a strong federal government.

9. b.

The author says that the house on Pine Street "had enough space inside but didn't have a big enough yard for [their] three dogs."

10. c.

Students who used private tutoring services increased their GPA by 0.7 points, which is more than the free tutoring service (0.3) or a combination of the two (0.5).

11. a.

The author writes, "But people who try to sell you this narrative are wrong. The Civil War was not a battle of cultural identities—it was a battle about slavery."

12. d.

The passage states that "the North had forged its own identity as a center of centralized commerce."

13. a.

The author writes that "[t]here's yet another class of symbiosis that is controversial among scientists" and goes on to say that "many scientists claim the relationships currently described as commensal are just mutualistic or parasitic in ways that haven't been discovered yet." This implies that scientists debate about the topic of commensalism.

14. b.

The author writes that "[a]s these communities have evolved, the species in them have developed complex, long-term interspecies interactions known as symbiotic relationships." She then goes on to describe the different types of symbiotic relationships that exist.

15. c.

The author writes that "tapeworms, which steal nutrients from their host, are parasitic."

SIX: LIFE SCIENCE

Biological Molecules

Molecules that contain carbon bound to hydrogen are **organic molecules**. Large organic molecules that contain many atoms and repeating units are **macromolecules**. Many macromolecules are **polymers** composed of repeating small units called **monomers**. There are four basic biological macromolecules that are common between all organisms: carbohydrates, lipids, proteins, and nucleic acids.

Carbohydrates, also called sugars, are polymers made of carbon, hydrogen, and oxygen atoms. The monomer for carbohydrates are **monosaccharides**, such as glucose and fructose, that combine to form more complex sugars called **polysaccharides**. Carbohydrates store energy and provide support to cellular structures.

Lipids, commonly known as fats, are composed mainly of hydrogen and carbon. They serve a number of functions depending on their particular structure: they make up the membrane of cells and can act as fuel, as steroids, and as hormones. Lipids are hydrophobic, meaning they repel water.

Proteins serve an incredibly wide variety of purposes within the body. As enzymes, they play key roles in important processes like DNA replication, cellular division, and cellular metabolism. Structural proteins provide rigidity to cartilage, hair, nails, and the cytoskeletons (the network of molecules that holds the parts of a cell in place). They are also involved in communication between cells and in the transportation of molecules.

 Did You Know? An **enzyme** is a protein that accelerates a specific chemical reaction.

Proteins are composed of individual **amino acids**, which are joined together by peptide bonds to form **polypeptides**. There are twenty amino acids, and the order of the amino acids in the polypeptide determines the shape and function of the molecule.

Nucleic acids store hereditary information and are composed of monomers called **nucleotides.** Each nucleotide includes a sugar, a phosphate group, and a nitrogenous base.

There are two types of nucleic acids. **Deoxyribonucleic acid (DNA)** contains the genetic instructions to produce proteins. It is composed of two strings of nucleotides wound into a double helix shape. The "backbone" of the helix is made from the nucleotide's sugar (deoxyribose) and phosphate groups. The "rungs" of the ladder are made from one of four nitrogenous bases: adenine, thymine, cytosine, and guanine. These bases bond together in specific pairs: adenine with thymine and cytosine with guanine.

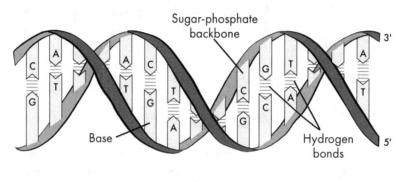

Figure 6.1. The Structure of DNA

Ribonucleic acid (RNA) transcribes information from DNA and plays several vital roles in the replication of DNA and the manufacturing of proteins. RNA nucleotides contain a sugar (ribose), a phosphate group, and one of four nitrogenous bases: adenine, uracil, cytosine, and guanine. It is usually found as a single-stranded molecule. There are three main differences between DNA and RNA:

1. DNA contains the nucleotide thymine; RNA contains the nucleotide uracil.
2. DNA is double-stranded; RNA is single-stranded.
3. DNA is made from the sugar deoxyribose; RNA is made from the sugar ribose.

PRACTICE QUESTIONS

1. The monomers that make up proteins are called

 a. monosaccharides

 b. nucleotides

 c. amino acids

 d. polypeptides

 e. enzymes

Answer:

c. Amino acid monomers are the building blocks of proteins.

2. Nucleic acids' primary purpose is to store
   a. carbon
   b. proteins
   c. water
   d. chemical energy
   e. genetic information

Answer:

e. Nucleic acids (DNA and RNA) store genetic information.

Nucleic Acids

DNA stores information by coding for proteins using blocks of three nucleotides called **codons**. Each codon codes for a specific amino acid; together, all the codons needed to make a specific protein are called a **gene**. In addition to codons for specific amino acids, there are also codons that signal "start" and "stop."

The production of a protein starts with **transcription**. During transcription, the two sides of the DNA helix unwind and a complementary strand of messenger RNA (mRNA) is manufactured using the DNA as a template.

This mRNA then travels outside the nucleus where it is "read" by a ribosome during **translation**. Each codon on the mRNA is matched to an anti-codon on a strand of tRNA, which carries a specific amino acid. The amino acids bond as they are lined up next to each other, forming a polypeptide.

When it is not being transcribed, DNA is tightly wound around proteins called **histones** to create **nucleosomes**, which are in turn packaged into **chromatin**. The structure of chromatin allows large amounts of DNA to be stored in a very small space and helps regulate transcription by controlling access to specific sections of DNA. Tightly folding the DNA also helps prevent damage to the genetic code. Chromatin is further bundled into packages of DNA called **chromosomes**. During cell division, DNA is replicated to create two identical copies of each chromosome called **chromatids**.

Somatic (body) cells are **diploid**, meaning they carry two copies of each chromosome—one inherited from each parent. Gametes, which are reproductive cells, are **haploid** and carry only one copy of each chromosome. Human somatic cells have forty-six chromosomes, while human egg and sperm each carry twenty-three chromosomes.

A **mutation** causes a change in the sequence of nucleotides within DNA. For example, the codon GAC codes for the amino acid aspartic acid. However, if the cytosine is swapped for adenine, the codon now reads GAA, which corresponds to the amino acid glutamic acid. Germ-line mutations, or mutations that occur in a cell that will become a gamete, can be passed on to the offspring of an organism. Somatic mutations cannot be passed on to the offspring of an organism.

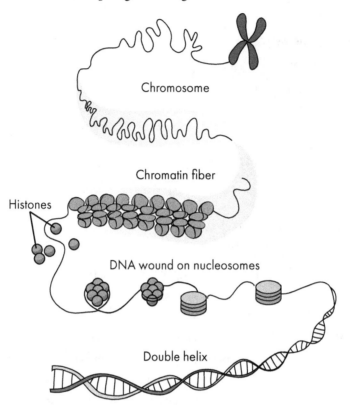

Figure 6.2. DNA, Chromatin, and Chromosomes

PRACTICE QUESTION

The information stored in RNA is used to produce a protein during

a. replication

b. translation

c. transcription

d. photosynthesis

e. respiration

Answer:

b. Translation is the process of matching codons in RNA to the correct anti-codon to manufacture a protein.

Structure and Function of Cells

A **cell** is the smallest unit of life that can reproduce on its own. Unicellular organisms, such as amoebae, are made up of only one cell, while multicellular organisms are comprised of many cells. There are two basic types of cells: prokaryotic and eukaryotic. **Prokaryotic cells**, which include most bacteria, do not have a nucleus. The DNA in a prokaryotic cell is carried in the **cytoplasm**, which is the fluid that makes up the volume of the cell. **Eukaryotic cells** contain a nucleus where genetic material is stored.

Cells contain smaller structures called **organelles** that perform specific functions within the cell. These include **mitochondria**, which produce energy; **ribosomes**, which produce proteins; and **vacuoles**, which store water and other molecules.

Plant cells include a number of structures not found in animal cells. These include the **cell wall**, which provides the cell with a hard outer structure, and **chloroplasts**, where photosynthesis occurs.

The outer surface of human cells is made up of a **plasma membrane**, which gives the cell its shape. This membrane is primarily composed of a **phospholipid bilayer**, which itself is made up of two layers of lipids that face opposing directions. This functions to separate the inner cellular environment from the extracellular space, the space between cells. Molecules travel through the cell membrane using a number of different methods:

+ **Diffusion** occurs when molecules pass through the membrane from areas of high to low concentration.

+ **Facilitated diffusion** occurs with the assistance of proteins embedded in the membrane.

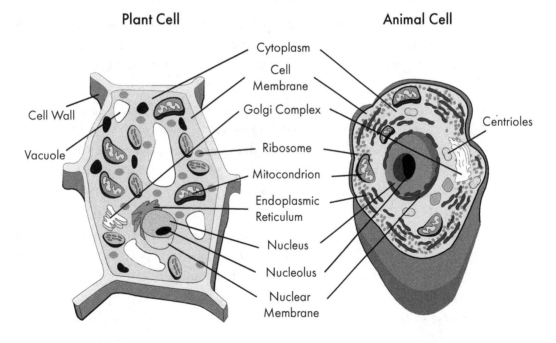

Figure 6.3. Cell Organelles

- **Osmosis** is the movement of water from areas of high to low concentration.
- During **active transport**, proteins in the membrane use energy (in the form of ATP) to move molecules across the membrane.

PRACTICE QUESTION

The structure that stores genetic material in a cell is the

a. nucleus

b. chloroplast

c. ribosome

d. vacuole

e. mitochondrion

Answer:

a. Genetic material (DNA) is stored in the nucleus.

Cellular Respiration

Organisms use chains of chemical reactions called **biochemical pathways** to acquire, store, and use energy. The molecule most commonly used to store energy is **adenosine triphosphate (ATP)**. When a phosphate group (Pi) is removed from ATP, creating **adenosine diphosphate (ADP)**, energy is released. The cell harnesses this energy to perform processes such as transport, growth, and replication.

Cells also transfer energy using the molecules **nicotinamide adenine dinucleotide phosphate (NADPH)** and **nicotinamide adenine dinucleotide (NADH)**. These molecules are generally used to carry energy-rich electrons during the process of creating ATP.

In **cellular respiration,** food molecules such as glucose are broken down, and the electrons harvested from these molecules are used to make ATP. The first stage of cellular respiration is an **anaerobic** (does not require oxygen) process called **glycolysis.** Glycolysis takes place in the cytoplasm of a cell and transforms glucose into two molecules of pyruvate. In the process, two molecules of ATP and two molecules of NADH are produced.

Under anaerobic conditions, pyruvate is reduced to acids and sometimes gases and/ or alcohols in a process called **fermentation.** However, this process is less efficient than aerobic cellular respiration and produces only two ATP.

Under aerobic conditions, pyruvate enters the second stage of cellular respiration— the **Krebs cycle.** The Krebs cycle takes place in the mitochondria, or tubular organelles, of a eukaryotic cell. Here, pyruvate is oxidized completely to form six molecules of carbon dioxide (CO_2). This set of reactions also produces two more molecules of ATP, ten molecules of NADH, and two molecules of $FADH_2$ (an electron carrier).

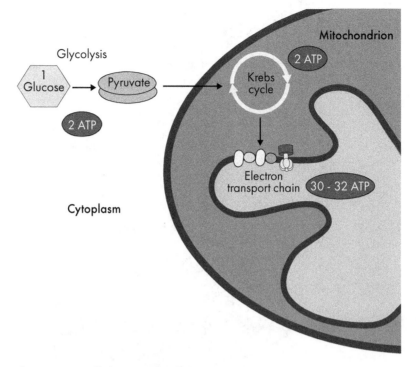

Figure 6.4. Cellular Respiration

The electrons carried by NADH and $FADH_2$ are transferred to the **electron transport chain,** where they cascade through carrier molecules embedded in the inner mitochondrial membrane. Oxygen is the final electron receptor in the chain; it reacts with these electrons and hydrogen to form water. This sequential movement of electrons drives the formation of a proton (H^+) gradient, which is used by the enzyme ATP synthase to produce ATP. The electron transport chain produces thirty to thirty-two molecules of ATP.

The balanced chemical equation for cellular respiration is:

$$C_6H_{12}O_6 + 6O_2 \rightarrow 6CO_2 + 6H_2O$$

PRACTICE QUESTION

The stage of cellular respiration that produces the largest number of ATP molecules is

a. glycolysis

b. fermentation

c. the Krebs cycle

d. the electron transport chain

e. the citric acid cycle

Answer:

d. The electron transport chain produces thirty to thirty-two molecules of ATP made during cellular respiration. The other choices each produce only two molecules of ATP.

Photosynthesis

The sun powers nearly all biological systems on this planet. Plants, along with some bacteria and algae, harness the energy of sunlight and transform it into chemical energy through the process of **photosynthesis.**

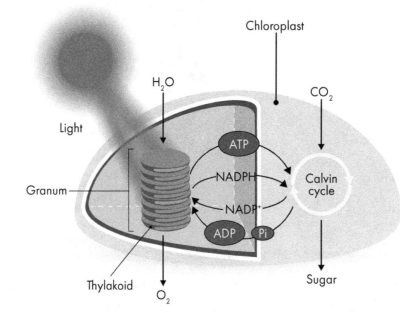

Figure 6.5. Photosynthesis

Inside each chloroplast are stacks of flat, interconnected sacs called **thylakoids.** Within the membrane of each thylakoid sac are light-absorbing pigments called **chlorophyll.**

In the light-dependent reactions of photosynthesis, light penetrates the chloroplast and strikes the chlorophyll. The energy in the sunlight excites electrons, boosting them to a higher energy level. These excited electrons then cascade through the **electron transport chain**, creating energy in the form of ATP and NADPH. This reaction also splits water to release O_2.

The ATP and NADPH created by the light-dependent stage of photosynthesis enter the **Calvin cycle**, which uses the energy to produce the carbohydrate glucose ($C_6H_{12}O_6$). The carbon needed for this reaction comes from atmospheric CO_2.

The balanced chemical equation for photosynthesis is:

$$6CO_2 + 6H_2O \rightarrow C_6H_{12}O_6 + 6O_2$$

Glucose is produced during the Calvin cycle using

a. O_2

b. CO_2

c. ADP

d. H_2

e. N_2

Answer:

b. During the Calvin cycle, carbon dioxide (CO_2) is used to produce glucose.

Cell Division

The process of cell growth and reproduction is the **cell cycle**. Eukaryotic cells spend the majority of their lifespan in **interphase**, during which the cell performs necessary functions and grows. During interphase, the cell also copies its DNA. Then, during **mitosis** the two identical sets of DNA are pulled to opposite sides of the cell. The cell then splits during **cytokinesis**, resulting in two cells that have identical copies of the original cell's DNA.

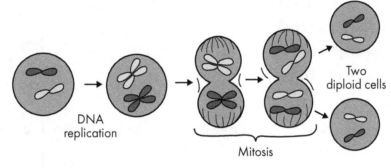

Figure 6.6. Mitosis

Meiosis is the process of sexual reproduction, or the formation of gametes (egg and sperm cells). During meiosis, the replicated DNA is separated to form two diploid cells. These cells in turn will separate again, with each cell retaining a single set of chromosomes. The result is four haploid cells.

CONTINUE

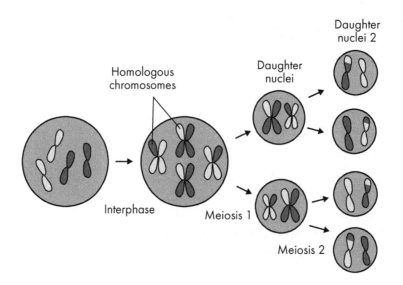

Figure 6.7. Meiosis

PRACTICE QUESTION

The result of mitosis and cytokinesis is

a. two haploid cells

b. four haploid cells

c. eight haploid cells

d. two diploid cells

e. four diploid cells

Answer:

d. The daughter cells produced during mitosis are genetically identical to their diploid (2n) parent.

Genetics

Genetics is the study of heredity—how characteristics are passed from parents to offspring. These characteristics, or traits, are determined by genes. Each individual has two versions of the same gene, called **alleles**, with one contributed by each parent. An individual is **homozygous** for a particular gene if both alleles are the same, and **heterozygous** if the two alleles are different.

 Helpful Hint: Alleles are written as a single letter with the dominant allele capitalized (A) and the recessive allele lowercase (a).

For a particular gene, the **dominant** allele will always be expressed, and the **recessive** allele will only be expressed if the other allele is also recessive. In other words, a recessive trait is only expressed if the individual is homozygous for that allele.

The full set of genetic material in an organism is its **genotype**. The organism's **phenotype** is the set of observable traits in the organism. For example, brown hair is a phenotype. The genotype of this trait is a set of alleles that contain the genetic information for brown hair.

The genotype, and resulting phenotype, of sexually reproducing organisms can be tracked using **Punnett squares**, which show the alleles of the parent generation on each of two axes. The possible genotypes of the resulting offspring, called the F1 generation, are then shown in the body of the square.

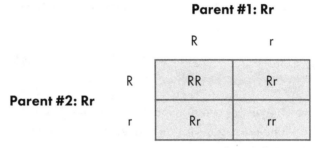

Figure 6.8. Punnett Square

In Figure 6.8., two heterozygous parents for trait R are mated, resulting in the following genotypes and phenotypes for the offspring:

- ✦ 1 homozygous dominant (dominant phenotype)
- ✦ 2 heterozygous (dominant phenotype)
- ✦ 1 homozygous recessive (recessive phenotype)

> 🔍 Did You Know? Many of the rules of genetics were discovered by Gregor Mendel, a nineteenth-century abbot who used pea plants to show how traits are passed down through generations.

Non-Mendelian inheritance describes patterns that do not follow the ratios described above. These patterns can occur for a number of reasons. Alleles might show **incomplete dominance**, where one allele is not fully expressed over the other, resulting in a third phenotype (for example, a red flower and white flower cross to create a pink flower). Alleles can also be **codominant**, meaning both are fully expressed (such as the AB blood type).

The expression of genes can also be regulated by mechanisms other than the dominant/recessive relationship. For example, some genes may inhibit the expression of other genes, a process called **epistasis**. The environment can also impact gene expression. For example, organisms with the same genotype may grow to different sizes depending on the nutrients available to them.

1. The dominant allele will not be expressed when

   a. a recessive allele from the father is paired with a recessive allele from the mother

   b. a dominant allele from the father is paired with a dominant allele from the mother

   c. a dominant allele from the father is paired with a recessive allele from the mother

   d. a recessive allele from the father is paired with a dominant allele from the mother

   e. a recessive allele from the father is paired with no allele from the mother

   Answer:

   a. This genotype is homozygous, and the recessive trait is the only trait that can be expressed.

2. Alleles for brown eyes (B) are dominant over alleles for blue eyes (b). If two parents are both heterozygous for this gene, the percent chance that their offspring will have brown eyes is

   a. 0 percent

   b. 25 percent

   c. 50 percent

   d. 75 percent

   e. 100 percent

   Answer:

   d. The Punnett square shows that there is a 75 percent chance the child will have the dominant B gene, and thus have brown eyes.

	B	b
B	BB	Bb
b	Bb	bb

Evolution

Evolution is the gradual genetic change in species over time. Natural selection alters the variation and frequency of certain alleles and phenotypes within a population.

This increased variation and frequency leads to varying reproductive success, in which individuals with certain traits survive over others. Combined, these mechanisms lead to gradual changes in the genotype of individual populations that, over time, can result in the creation of a new species.

Natural selection is a process in which only the members of a population best adapted to their environment tend to survive and reproduce, which ensures that their favorable traits will be passed on to future generations of the species. There are four basic conditions that must be met in order for natural selection to occur:

1. inherited variation
2. overproduction of offspring
3. fitness to environment
4. differential reproduction

? Check Your Understanding: Why might a harmful mutation continue to exist in a population?

The offspring with inherited variations best suited for their environment will be more likely to survive than others and are therefore more likely to pass on their successful genes to future populations through reproduction. This is referred to as **fitness**. An organism that is considered biologically "fit" will be more successful passing on its genes through reproduction compared to other members of the population. The frequency of certain alleles in a gene pool will change as a result.

Artificial selection occurs in a species when humans get involved in the reproductive process. Over time, humans have intentionally bred organisms with the same desirable traits in a process called selective breeding. This has led to the evolution of many common crops and farm animals that are bred specifically for human consumption, as well as among domesticated animals, such as horses or dogs.

PRACTICE QUESTION

Natural selection is NOT occurring when

a. peahens select the most brightly colored peacocks as mates

b. large bears chase smaller rivals away from food sources

c. sparrows with a certain beak shape reach plentiful food sources

d. farmers plant seeds only from the most productive corn plants

e. male ibex use their horns to fight other males before mating with females

Answer:

d. Farmers choosing specific traits in plants is an example of artificial selection.

Ecology

Ecology is the study of organisms' interactions with each other and the environment. Ecologists break down the groups of organisms and abiotic features into hierarchal groups.

Groups of organisms of the same species living in the same geographic area are called **populations**. These organisms will compete with each other for resources and mates and will display characteristic patterns in growth related to their interactions with the environment. For example, many populations exhibit a carrying capacity, which is the highest number of individuals that the resources in a given environment can support. Populations that outgrow their carrying capacity are likely to experience increased death rates until the population reaches a stable level again.

Populations of different species living together in the same geographic region are called **communities**. Within a community there are many different interactions among individuals of different species. **Predators** consume **prey** for food, and some species are in **competition** for the same limited pool of resources. In a **symbiotic** relationship, two species have evolved to share a close relationship. Two species may also have a **parasitic** relationship in which one organism benefits to the detriment of the other, such as ticks feeding off a dog. Both species benefit in a **mutualistic** relationship, and in a **commensalistic** relationship, one species benefits and the other feels the effects.

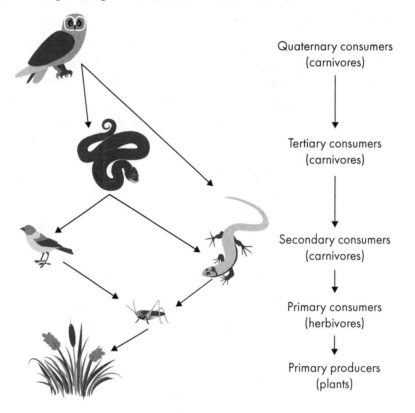

Figure 6.9. Food Web

Within a community, a species exists in a **food web**: every species either consumes or is consumed by another (or others). The lowest trophic level in the web is occupied by **producers**, which include plants and algae that produce energy directly from the sun. The next level are **primary consumers** (herbivores), which consume plant matter. The next trophic level includes **secondary consumers** (carnivores), which consume herbivores.

A food web may also contain another level of **tertiary consumers** (carnivores that consume other carnivores). In a real community, these webs can be extremely complex, with species existing on multiple trophic levels. Communities also include **decomposers**, which are organisms that break down dead matter.

The collection of biotic (living) and abiotic (nonliving) features in a geographic area is called an **ecosystem**. For example, in a forest, the ecosystem consists of all the organisms (animals, plants, fungi, bacteria, etc.), in addition to the soil, groundwater, rocks, and other abiotic features.

Biomes are collections of plant and animal communities that exist within specific climates. They are similar to ecosystems, but they do not include abiotic components and can exist within and across continents. For example, the Amazon rainforest is a specific ecosystem, while tropical rainforests in general are considered a biome that includes a set of similar communities across the world. Together, all the living and nonliving parts of the earth are known as the **biosphere**.

Terrestrial biomes are usually defined by distinctive patterns in temperature and rainfall, and aquatic biomes are defined by the type of water and organisms found there. Examples of biomes include:

+ **deserts**: extreme temperatures and very low rainfall with specialized vegetation and small mammals
+ **tropical rainforests**: hot and wet with an extremely high diversity of species
+ **temperate grasslands**: moderate precipitation and distinct seasons with grasses and shrubs dominating
+ **temperate forests**: moderate precipitation and temperatures with deciduous trees dominating
+ **tundra**: extremely low temperatures and short growing seasons with little or no tree growth
+ **coral reefs**: a marine (saltwater) system with high levels of diversity
+ **lake**: an enclosed body of fresh water

If the delicate balance of an ecosystem is disrupted, the system may not function properly. For example, if all the secondary consumers disappear, the population of primary consumers would increase, causing the primary consumers to overeat the producers and eventually starve. **Keystone species** are especially important in a particular community, and removing them decreases the overall diversity of the ecosystem.

1. An abiotic environmental factor that influences population size is

    a. food availability

    b. rate of precipitation

    c. mutualism

    d. competition

    e. predation

    Answer:

    b. Precipitation is a nonliving (abiotic) factor that influences population size.

2. The terrestrial biome characterized by moderate rainfall and the dominance of deciduous trees is called

    a. desert

    b. tropical rainforest

    c. temperate forest

    d. tundra

    e. grasslands

    Answer:

    c. Temperate forests have moderate rainfall and are dominated by deciduous trees.

Human Anatomy and Physiology

In a multicellular organism, cells are grouped together into **tissues**, and these tissues are grouped into **organs**, which perform specific **functions**. The heart, for example, is the organ that pumps blood throughout the body. Organs are further grouped into **organ systems**, such as the digestive or respiratory systems.

Anatomy is the study of the structure of organisms, and **physiology** is the study of how these structures function. Both disciplines study the systems that allow organisms to perform a number of crucial functions, including the exchange of energy, nutrients, and waste products with the environment. This exchange allows organisms to maintain **homeostasis**, or the stabilization of internal conditions.

> Helpful Hint: In science, a **system** is a collection of interconnected parts that make up a complex whole with defined boundaries. Systems may be closed, meaning nothing passes in or out of them, or open, meaning they have inputs and outputs.

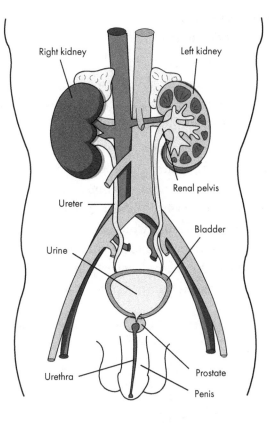

Figure 6.10. Genitourinary System

The human body has a number of systems that perform vital functions, including the digestive, excretory, respiratory, circulatory, skeletal, muscular, immune, nervous, endocrine, and reproductive systems.

The **digestive system** breaks food down into nutrients for use by the body's cells. Food enters through the **mouth** and moves through the **esophagus** to the **stomach**, where it is physically and chemically broken down. The food particles then move into the **small intestine**, where the majority of nutrients are absorbed. Finally, the remaining particles enter the **large intestine**, which mostly absorbs water, and waste exits through the **rectum** and **anus**. This system also includes other organs, such as the **liver**, **gallbladder**, and **pancreas**, that manufacture substances needed for digestion.

The **genitourinary system** removes waste products from the body. Its organs include the liver, which breaks down harmful substances, and the **kidneys**, which filter waste from the bloodstream. The excretory system also includes the **bladder** and **urinary tract**, which expel the waste filtered by

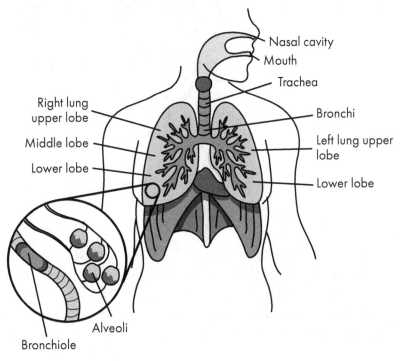

Figure 6.11. Respiratory System

the kidneys; the lungs, which expel the carbon dioxide created by cellular metabolism; and the skin, which secretes salt in the form of perspiration.

The **respiratory system** takes in oxygen (which is needed for cellular functioning) and expels carbon dioxide. Humans take in air primarily through the nose but also through the mouth. This air travels down the **trachea** and **bronchi** into the **lungs**, which are composed of millions of small structures called alveoli that allow for the exchange of gases between the blood and the air.

The circulatory system carries oxygen, nutrients, and waste products in the blood to and from all the cells of the body. The **heart** is a four-chambered muscle that pumps blood throughout the body. The four chambers are the right atrium, right ventricle, left atrium, and left ventricle. Deoxygenated blood (blood from which all the oxygen has been extracted and used) enters the right atrium and then is sent from the right ventricle through the pulmonary artery to the lungs, where it collects oxygen. The oxygen-rich blood then returns to the left atrium of the heart and is pumped out the left ventricle to the rest of the body.

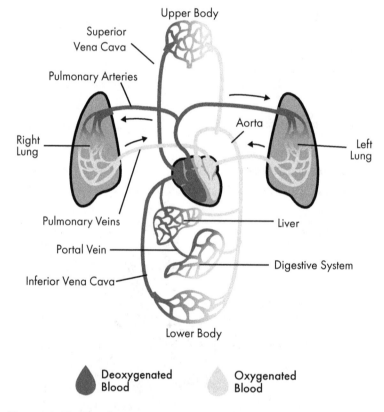

Figure 6.12. Circulatory System

Blood travels through a system of vessels. **Arteries** branch directly off the heart and carry blood away from it. The largest artery is the aorta, which carries blood from the heart to the rest of the body. **Veins** carry blood back to the heart from other parts of the body. Most veins carry deoxygenated blood, but the pulmonary veins carry oxygenated blood from the lungs back to the heart to then be pumped to the rest of the body.

Arteries and veins branch into smaller and smaller vessels until they become **capillaries**, which are the smallest vessels and the site where gas exchange occurs.

The **skeletal system**, which is composed of the body's **bones** and **joints**, provides support for the body and helps with movement. Bones also store some of the body's nutrients and produce specific types of cells. Humans are born with 237 bones. However, many of these bones fuse during childhood, and adults have only 206 bones. Bones can have a rough or smooth texture and come in four basic shapes: long, flat, short, and irregular.

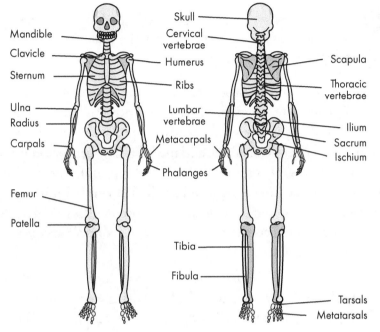

Figure 6.13. The Skeletal System

The **muscular system** allows the body to move and also moves blood and other substances through the body. The human body has three types of muscles. Skeletal muscles are voluntary muscles (meaning they can be controlled) that are attached to bones and move the body. Smooth muscles are involuntary muscles (meaning they cannot be controlled) that create movement in parts of the digestive tract, blood vessels, and the reproduction system. Finally, cardiac muscle is the involuntary muscle that contracts the heart, pumping blood throughout the body.

> Did You Know? Some skeletal muscles, such as the diaphragm and those that control blinking, can be voluntarily controlled but usually operate involuntarily.

The **immune system** protects the body from infection by foreign particles and organisms. It includes the **skin** and mucous membranes, which act as physical barriers, and a number of specialized cells that destroy foreign substances in the body. The human body has an adaptive immune system, meaning it can recognize and respond to foreign substances once it has been exposed to them. This is the underlying mechanism behind vaccines.

The immune system is composed of **B cells**, or B lymphocytes, that produce special proteins called **antibodies** that bind to foreign substances, called **antigens**, and neutralize them. **T cells**, or T lymphocytes, remove body cells that have been infected by foreign invaders like bacteria or viruses. **Helper T cells** coordinate production of antibodies by B cells and removal of infected cells by T cells. **Killer T cells** destroy body cells that have been infected by invaders after they are identified and removed by T cells. Finally, **memory cells** remember antigens that have been removed so the immune system can respond more quickly if they enter the body again.

> Did You Know? Memory B cells are the underlying mechanisms behind vaccines, which introduce a harmless version of a pathogen into the body to activate the body's adaptive immune response.

The **nervous system** processes external stimuli and sends signals throughout the body. It is made up of two parts. The central nervous system (CNS) includes the brain and spinal cord and is where information is processed and stored. The brain has three parts: the cerebrum, cerebellum, and medulla. The **cerebrum** is the biggest part of the brain, the wrinkly gray part at the front and top, and controls different functions like thinking, vision, hearing, touch, and smell. The **cerebellum** is located at the back and bottom of the brain and controls motor movements. The **medulla**, or brain stem, is where the brain connects to the spinal cord and controls automatic body functions like breathing and heartbeat.

The peripheral nervous system (PNS) includes small cells called **neurons** that transmit information throughout the body using electrical signals. Neurons are made up of three basic parts: the cell body, dendrites, and axons. The cell body is the main part of the cell where the organelles are located. Dendrites are long arms that extend from the main cell body and communicate with other cells' dendrites through chemical messages passed across a space called a synapse. Axons are extensions from the cell body and transmit messages to the muscles.

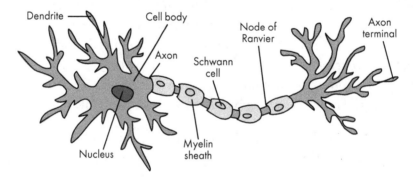

Figure 6.14. Neuron

The **endocrine system** is a collection of organs that produce **hormones**, which are chemicals that regulate bodily processes. These organs include the pituitary gland, hypothalamus, pineal gland, thyroid gland, parathyroid glands, adrenal glands, testes (in males), ovaries (in females), and the placenta (in pregnant females). Together, the hormones these organs produce regulate a wide variety of bodily functions, including hunger, sleep, mood, reproduction, and temperature. Some organs that are part of other systems can also act as endocrine organs, including the pancreas and liver.

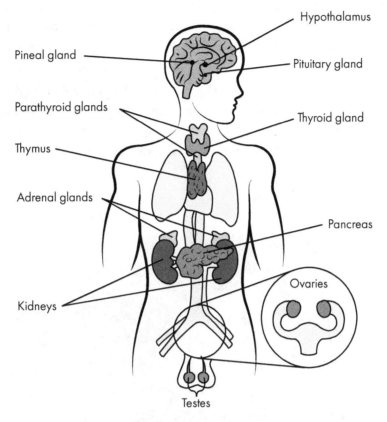

Figure 6.15. Endocrine System

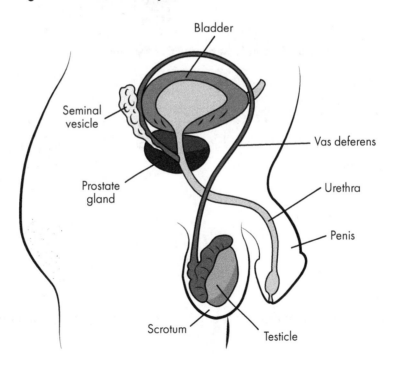

Figure 6.16. Male Reproductive System

The reproductive system includes the organs necessary for sexual reproduction. In males, sperm is produced in the **testes** (also known as **testicles**) and carried through a thin tube called the **vas deferens** to the **urethra**, which carries sperm through the **penis** and out of the body. The **prostate** is a muscular gland approximately the size of a walnut that is located between the male bladder and penis and produces a fluid that nourishes and protects sperm.

In the female reproductive system, eggs are produced in the **ovaries** and released roughly once a month to move through the **fallopian tubes** to the **uterus**. If an egg is fertilized, the new embryo implants in the lining of the uterus and develops over the course of about nine months. At the end of **gestation**, the baby leaves the uterus through the cervix, and exits the body through the **vagina**. If the egg is not fertilized, the uterus will shed its lining.

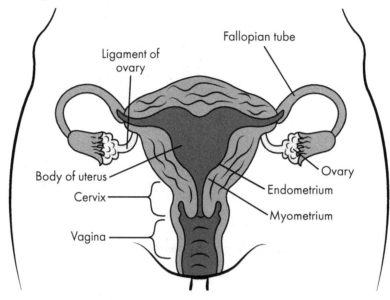

Figure 6.17. Female Reproductive System

PRACTICE QUESTIONS

1. The small bones in the hands are known as the

    a. tarsals

    b. ribs

    c. metatarsals

    d. vertebrae

    e. phalanges

    Answer:

    e. The small bones in the fingers of the hands are the phalanges.

2.   In the digestive tract, most of the nutrients are absorbed in the

   a.   small intestine

   b.   rectum

   c.   stomach

   d.   large intestine

   e.   esophagus

   Answer:

   a.   Most nutrients are absorbed by the small intestine.

Test Your Knowledge

Read the question, and then choose the most correct answer.

1. Which of the following is NOT a nucleobase of DNA?

   a. adenine

   b. guanine

   c. thymine

   d. uracil

2. Which of the following is a monomer used to build carbohydrates?

   a. glucose

   b. thymine

   c. aspartic acid

   d. histone

3. Which of the following processes uses the information stored in RNA to produce a protein?

   a. replication

   b. translation

   c. transcription

   d. mutation

4. The information stored in DNA is used to make which of the following molecules?

   a. amino acids

   b. proteins

   c. fatty acids

   d. monosaccharides

5. Which of the following is NOT present in an animal cell?

   a. nucleus

   b. mitochondria

   c. cytoplasm

   d. cell wall

6. Which of the following cell organelles are the site of lipid synthesis?

   a. smooth endoplasmic reticulum

   b. ribosome

   c. rough endoplasmic reticulum

   d. Golgi apparatus

7. Which of the following cellular processes does NOT use ATP?

   a. facilitated diffusion

   b. DNA replication

   c. active transport through the cell membrane

   d. movement of the mot complex in a flagellum

8. Which of the following molecules can be found in abundance in a fatigued muscle?

   a. glucose

   b. lactic acid

   c. ATP

   d. myoglobin

9. Why do some photosynthetic structures, like leaves, appear green?

   a. The epidermis of the leaf absorbs red and blue light.

   b. The epidermis of the leaf absorbs green light.

   c. The chlorophyll of the leaf absorbs red and blue light.

   d. The chlorophyll of the leaf absorbs green light.

10. The Calvin cycle produces one molecule of glucose from which of the following three molecules?

a. ATP, NADPH, and O_2

b. ATP, NADPH, and CO_2

c. CO_2, H_2O, and ATP

d. CO_2, H_2O, and O_2

11. The result of meiosis and cytokinesis is

a. two haploid (1n) cells.

b. four haploid (1n) cells.

c. two diploid (2n) cells.

d. four diploid (2n) cells.

12. Alleles for brown eyes (B) are dominant over alleles for blue eyes (b). If two parents are both heterozygous for this gene, what is the percent chance that their offspring will have brown eyes?

a. 25

b. 50

c. 75

d. 100

13. If a plant that is homozygous dominant (T) for a trait is crossed with a plant that is homozygous recessive (t) for the same trait, what will be the phenotype of the offspring if the trait follows Mendelian patterns of inheritance?

a. All offspring will show the dominant phenotype.

b. All offspring will show the recessive phenotype.

c. Half the offspring will show the dominant trait, and the other half will show the recessive phenotype.

d. All the offspring will show a mix of the dominant and recessive phenotypes.

14. A female who carries the recessive color blindness gene mates with a color-blind male, resulting in a male child. Which of the following numbers represents the likelihood the offspring will also be color blind?

a. 25 percent

b. 50 percent

c. 100 percent

d. 0 percent

15. Type AB blood—the expression of both A and B antigens on a red blood cell surface—occurs as the result of which of the following?

a. incomplete dominance

b. recombination

c. codominance

d. independent assortment

16. Which of the following is NOT a condition of natural selection?

a. differential reproduction

b. competition between species

c. overproduction of offspring

d. inheritance of traits

17. Which of the following is the type of nonrandom mating that leads to changes in allele frequency?

a. sexual selection

b. genetic drift

c. migration

d. gene flow

18. Which of the following aquatic biomes are located where freshwater streams empty into the ocean?

a. wetlands

b. coral reef

c. estuaries

d. littoral

19. Which of the following scenarios accurately describes primary succession?

 a. The ground is scorched by a lava flow; later the establishment of lichens begins on the volcanic rock, leading to the eventual formation of soils.

 b. A meadow is destroyed by a flood; eventually small grasses begin to grow again to begin establishing a healthy meadow ecosystem.

 c. A fire destroys a section of a forest; once the ashes clear, small animals begin making their homes within the area.

 d. A farmer overuses the land causing all the minerals and nutrients in the soil to be used up. Some leftover grass seeds in the soil begin to sprout, repopulating the land.

20. A barnacle is attached to the outside of the whale to collect and consume particulate matter as the whale moves through the ocean. The barnacle benefits, while the whale is unaffected. The phenomenon described is an example of

 a. predation

 b. commensalism

 c. mutualism

 d. parasitism

21. Which of the following organisms generate their own food through photosynthesis and make up the first level of the energy pyramid?

 a. heterotrophs

 b. autotrophs

 c. producers

 d. consumers

22. Which of the following is composed only of members of the same species?

 a. ecosystem

 b. community

 c. biome

 d. population

23. Which of the following type of muscle is responsible for voluntary movement in the body?

 a. cardiac

 b. visceral

 c. smooth

 d. skeletal

24. Which of the following organs is an accessory organ that food does NOT pass through as part of digestion?

 a. pharynx

 b. mouth

 c. small intestine

 d. liver

25. Which of the following is NOT a function of the respiratory system in humans?

 a. to exchange gas

 b. to produce sound and speech

 c. to distribute oxygen to the rest of the body

 d. to remove particles from the air

ANSWER KEY

1. d.

Uracil (U) is a pyrimidine found in RNA, replacing the thymine (T) pyrimidine found in DNA.

2. a.

Glucose is a monosaccharide that can be used to build larger polysaccharides.

3. b.

Translation is a process of matching codons in RNA to the correct anti-codon to manufacture a protein.

4. b.

Proteins are the expressed products of a gene.

5. d.

The cell wall is the structure that gives plant cells their rigidity.

6. a.

The smooth endoplasmic reticulum is a series of membranes attached to the cell nucleus and plays an important role in the production and storage of lipids. It is called smooth because it lacks ribosomes on the membrane surface.

7. a.

Facilitated diffusion is a form of passive transport across the cell membrane and does not use energy.

8. b.

Lactic acid, a byproduct of anaerobic respiration, builds up in muscles and causes fatigue. This occurs when the energy exerted by the muscle exceeds the amount of oxygen available for aerobic respiration.

9. c.

Light passes through the epidermis and strikes the pigment chlorophyll, which absorbs the wavelengths of light that humans see as red and blue and reflects the wavelengths of light that the human eye perceives as green.

10. b.

Glucose is produced from CO_2 by the energy stored in ATP and the hydrogen atoms associated with NADPH.

11. b.

Four haploid (1n) cells are produced during meiosis.

12. c.

The Punnett square shows that there is a 75 percent chance the child will have the dominant B gene, and thus have brown eyes.

	B	b
B	BB	Bb
b	Bb	bb

13. a.

Because each offspring will inherit the dominant allele, all the offspring will show the dominant phenotype. The offspring would only show a mix of the two phenotypes if they did not follow Mendelian inheritance patterns.

14. b.

The offspring has a 50 percent chance of inheriting the dominant allele and a 50 percent chance of inheriting the recessive allele from his mother.

15. c.

Type AB blood occurs when two equally dominant alleles (A and B) are inherited. Since they are both dominant, one does not mask the other; instead, both are expressed.

16. b.

Competition between species is not necessary for natural selection to occur, although it can influence the traits that are selected for within a population.

17. a.

Sexual selection changes allele frequency because it leads to some members of the population reproducing more frequently than others.

18. c.

Estuaries are found at the boundary of ocean and stream biomes and are very ecologically productive areas.

19. a.

Primary succession can only occur on newly exposed earth that was not previously inhabited by living things. Often this new land is the result of lava flows or glacial movement.

20. b.

In a commensal relationship, one species benefits with no impact on the other.

21. c.

Producers are a kind of autotroph that are found on the energy pyramid and produce food via photosynthesis.

22. d.

A population is all the members of the same species in a given area.

23. d.

Skeletal muscles are attached to the skeletal system and are controlled voluntarily.

24. d.

The liver is an accessory organ that detoxifies ingested toxins and produces bile for fat digestion.

25. c.

The cardiovascular system distributes oxygen to the rest of the body.

SEVEN: PHYSICAL SCIENCE

The Structure of the Atom

All matter is composed of very small particles called **atoms**. Atoms can be further broken down into subatomic particles. **Protons**, which are positive, and **neutrons**, which are neutral, form the nucleus of the atom. Negative particles called **electrons** orbit the nucleus.

While electrons are often depicted as orbiting the nucleus like a planet orbits the sun, they're actually arranged in cloud-like areas called **shells**. The shells closest to the nucleus have the lowest energy and are filled first. The high-energy shells farther from the nucleus only fill with electrons once lower-energy shells are full.

The outermost electron shell of an atom is its **valence shell**. The electrons in this shell are involved in chemical reactions. Atoms are most stable when their valence shell is full (usually with eight electrons), so the atom will lose, gain, or share electrons to fill its valence shell.

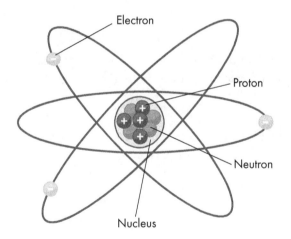

Figure 7.1. Structure of the Atom

A neutral atom will have an equal number of protons and electrons. When a neutral atom loses or gains electrons, it gains or loses charge accordingly, forming an **ion**. An ion with more protons than electrons has a positive charge and is called a **cation**. An ion with more electrons than protons has a negative charge and is considered an **anion**.

 Helpful Hint: The attractive and repulsive forces in an atom follow the universal law that "like charges repel and opposite charges attract."

For example, the element oxygen (O) has eight protons and eight electrons. A neutral oxygen atom is represented simply as O. However, if it gains two electrons, it becomes an anion with a charge of –2 and is written as O^{2-}.

All atoms with the same number of protons are the same **element** and cannot be further reduced to a simpler substance by chemical processes. Each element has a symbol, which is a one- or two-letter abbreviation for the element's name. The number of protons in an atom is that atom's **atomic number.**

Did You Know? Many element symbols are derived from the Latin names for elements. For example, the Latin name for *gold* is *aurum*, and its symbol is Au.

Along with atomic charge, atoms have measurable mass. Protons and neutrons are significantly more massive than electrons (about 1,800 times), so the mass of electrons is not considered when calculating the mass of an atom. Thus, an element's **mass number** is the number of protons and neutrons present in its atoms.

PRACTICE QUESTIONS

1. An atom with five protons and seven electrons has a charge of
   a. −12
   b. −2
   c. 2
   d. 5
   e. 12

   Answer:
   b. The total charge of an atom is the difference between the number of protons and electrons. Subtract the number of electrons from the number of protons: $5 - 7 = -2$.

2. The ion with the greatest number of electrons is
   a. K^+
   b. Cl^-
   c. Ca^+
   d. P^{3-}
   e. S^{2-}

   Answer:
   c. Calcium has an atomic number of 20 (found on the periodic table), meaning it has twenty protons. For a Ca ion to have a charge of 1+, it must have nineteen electrons. All the other ions have eighteen electrons.

The Periodic Table of the Elements

Elements are arranged on the **Periodic Table of the Elements** by their atomic number, which increases from top to bottom and left to right on the table. Hydrogen, the first element on the periodic table, has one proton while helium, the second element, has two, and so on.

The rows of the periodic table are called **periods**, and the vertical columns are called **groups**. Each group contains elements with the same number of valence electrons, meaning the elements have similar chemical properties.

The majority of the elements in the periodic table are metals. Metals have the following properties:

+ They are hard, opaque, and shiny.
+ They are ductile and malleable.
+ They conduct electricity and heat.
+ With the exception of mercury, they are solids.

Metals begin on the left side of the periodic table and span across the middle of the table, almost all the way to the right side. Examples of metals include gold (Au), tin (Sn), and lead (Pb).

Nonmetals are elements that do not conduct electricity and tend to be more reactive than metals. They can be solids, liquids, or gases. The nonmetals are located on the right side of the periodic table. Examples of nonmetals include sulfur (S), hydrogen (H), and oxygen (O).

Metalloids, or semimetals, are elements that possess both metal and nonmetal characteristics. For example, some metalloids are shiny but do not conduct electricity well. Metalloids are located between the metals and nonmetals on the periodic table. Some examples of metalloids are boron (B), silicon (Si), and arsenic (As).

PRACTICE QUESTIONS

1. Bismuth is a

    a. metal

    b. nonmetal

    c. metalloid

    d. transition element

    e. noble gas

    Answer:

    a. Bismuth is a metal.

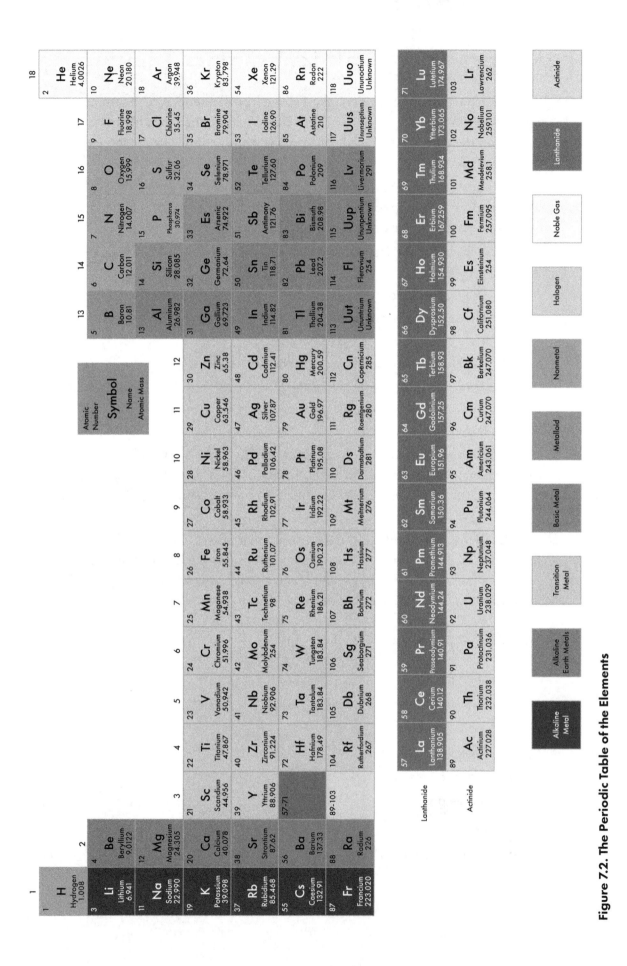

Figure 7.2. The Periodic Table of the Elements

2. Fluorine is most likely to form an ionic compound with

   a. nickel (Ni)

   b. beryllium (Be)

   c. sodium (Na)

   d. argon (Ar)

   e. chlorine (Cl)

   Answer:

   c. Fluorine forms the ion F⁻ and sodium forms the ion Na⁺. The two ions bond to form NaF.

Chemical Bonds

Chemical bonds are attractions between atoms that create molecules, which are substances consisting of more than one atom. There are three types of bonds: ionic, covalent, and metallic.

In an **ionic bond**, one atom "gives" its electrons to the other, resulting in one positively and one negatively charged atom. The bond is a result of the attraction between the two ions. Ionic bonds form between atoms on the left side of the periodic table (which will lose electrons) and those on the right side (which will gain electrons). Table salt (NaCl) is an example of a molecule held together by an ionic bond.

A **covalent bond** is created by a pair of atoms sharing electrons to fill their valence shells. In a **nonpolar** covalent bond, the electrons are shared evenly. In a **polar** covalent bond, the electrons are shared unevenly. One atom will exert a stronger pull on the shared electrons, giving that atom a slight negative charge. The other atom in the bond will have a slight positive charge. Water (H_2O) is an example of a polar molecule.

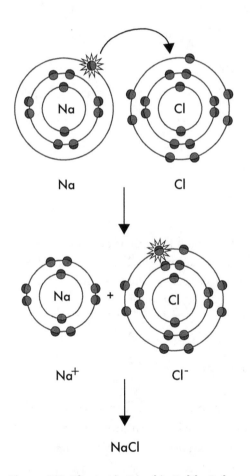

Na   Cl

Na⁺   Cl⁻

NaCl

Figure 7.3. The Ionic Bond in Table Salt

🔍 Did You Know? The polar nature of water is responsible for many of its unique properties. The small charges within a water molecule cause attraction between the molecules. The molecules then "stick" to each other (cohesion) and to other surfaces (adhesion).

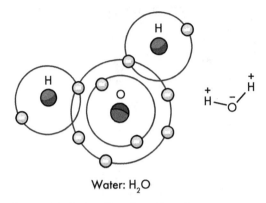

Water: H_2O

Figure 7.4. Polar Covalent Bond

Metals can form tightly packed arrays in which each atom is in close contact with many neighbors. The valence electrons are free to move between atoms and create a "sea" of delocalized charge. Any excitation, such as an electrical current, can cause the electrons to move throughout the array. The high electrical and thermal conductivity of metals is due to this ability of electrons to move throughout the lattice. This type of delocalized bonding is called **metallic bonding**.

PRACTICE QUESTION

A polar covalent bond joins the atoms in the molecule

a. LiF

b. CO2

c. H2

d. NaOH

e. O2

Answer:

b. Carbon and oxygen are both nonmetals that combine through a covalent bond. Oxygen has a strong pull on their shared electrons, so CO2 is polar. In hydrogen and oxygen gases, the identical atoms share electrons equally, so both compounds are nonpolar. Choices a and d are ionic compounds.

Properties of Matter

Matter is any substance that takes up space. The amount of matter in an object is that object's **mass**, which is measured in grams or kilograms. Mass is different from **weight**, which is a measure of the gravitational force exerted on an object. An object's mass never changes, but its weight will change if the gravitational force changes. The **density** of an object is the ratio of an object's mass to its volume.

Properties of substances are divided into two categories: physical and chemical. **Physical properties** are those that are measurable and can be seen without changing the chemical makeup of a substance. In contrast, **chemical properties** are those that determine how a substance will behave in a chemical reaction. Chemical properties cannot be identified simply by observing a material. Instead, the material must be engaged in a chemical reaction in order to identify its chemical properties. A **physical change** is a change in a substance's physical properties, and a **chemical change** is a change in its chemical properties.

Table 7.1. Properties of Matter

Physical Properties	Chemical Properties
mass	heat of combustion
temperature	flammability
density	toxicity
color	chemical stability
viscosity	enthalpy of formation

Helpful Hint: In both physical and chemical changes, matter is always conserved, meaning it can never be created or destroyed.

Temperature is the name given to the kinetic energy of all the atoms or molecules in a substance. While it might look like matter is not in motion, in fact, its atoms have kinetic energy and are constantly spinning and vibrating. The more energy the atoms have (meaning the more they spin and vibrate) the higher the substance's temperature.

Heat is the movement of energy from one substance to another. Energy will spontaneously move from high-energy (high-temperature) substances to low-energy (low-temperature) substances.

PRACTICE QUESTION

A substance that can change shape but not volume is a

a.   solid

b.   liquid

c.   gas

d.   solid or liquid

e.   liquid or gas

b. Liquids can change shape (for instance, when they are poured from one container into another) but not volume.

States of Matter

All matter exists in different **states** (or phases) that depend on the energy of the molecules in the matter. **Solid** matter has densely packed molecules and does not change volume or shape. **Liquids** have more loosely packed molecules and can change shape but not volume. **Gas** molecules are widely dispersed, and gases can change both shape and volume.

Changes in temperature and pressure can cause matter to change states. Generally, adding energy (in the form of heat) changes a substance to a higher energy state (e.g., solid to liquid). Transitions from a high to lower energy state (e.g., liquid to solid) release energy. Each of these changes has a specific name, summarized in the table below.

Table 7.2. Changes in State of Matter

Name	From	To	Occurs At	Enery Change
evaporation	liquid	gas	boiling point	uses energy
condensation	gas	liquid	boiling point	releases energy
melting	solid	liquid	freezing point	uses energy
freezing	liquid	solid	freezing point	releases energy
sublimation	solid	gas	---	uses energy
deposition	gas	solid	---	releases energy

PRACTICE QUESTION

The process that takes place when water reaches its boiling point is called

a. condensation

b. evaporation

c. melting

d. sublimation

e. freezing

Answer:

b. Evaporation is the process of conversion from liquid to gas that occurs at the boiling point.

Chemical Reactions

A **chemical reaction** occurs when one or more substances react to form new substances. **Reactants** are the substances that are consumed or altered in the chemical reaction, and the new substances are **products**. Equations are written with the reactants on the left, the products on the right, and an arrow between them. The state of the chemical compounds are sometimes noted using the labels s (solid), l (liquid), g (gas), or aq (aqueous, meaning a solution).

The equation below shows the reaction of hydrogen gas (H_2) and chlorine gas (Cl_2) to form hydrogen chloride (HCl), an acid.

$$H_2 \, (g) + Cl_2 \, (g) \rightarrow 2HCl \, (aq)$$

Chemical reactions follow the **law of conservation of matter**, which states that matter cannot be created or destroyed. In a reaction, the same types and numbers of atoms that appear on the left side must also appear on the right. To **balance** a chemical equation, coefficients (the numbers before the reactant or product) are added. In the equation above, a coefficient of two is needed on HCl so that two hydrogen and two chlorine atoms appear on each side of the arrow.

There are five main types of chemical reactions; these are summarized in the table below.

Table 7.3. Types of Reactions

Type of Reaction	General Formula	Example Reaction
Synthesis	$A + B \rightarrow C$	$2H_2 + O_2 \rightarrow 2H_2O$
Decomposition	$A \rightarrow B + C$	$2H_2O_2 \rightarrow 2H_2O + O_2$
Single displacement	$AB + C \rightarrow A + BC$	$CH_4 + Cl_2 \rightarrow CH_3Cl + HCl$
Double displacement	$AB + CD \rightarrow AC + BD$	$CuCl_2 + 2AgNo_3 \rightarrow Cu(NO_3)_2 + 2AgCl$
Combustion	$C_xH_y + O_2 \rightarrow CO_2 + H_2O$	$2C_8H_{18} + 25O_2 \rightarrow 16CO_2 + 18H_2O$

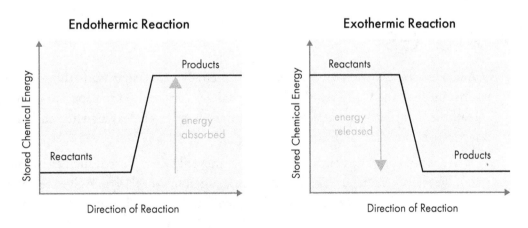

Figure 7.5. Stored Energy in Endothermic and Exothermic Reactions

Energy is required to break chemical bonds, and it is released when bonds form. The total energy absorbed or released during a chemical reaction will depend on the individual bonds being broken and formed. A reaction that releases energy is **exothermic**, and a reaction that absorbs energy is **endothermic**.

PRACTICE QUESTIONS

1. $Pb(NO_3)_2 + K_2CrO_4 \rightarrow PbCrO_4 + 2KNO_3$

The reaction shown above is a

    a.   combustion reaction

    b.   decomposition reaction

    c.   double-displacement reaction

    d.   single-replacement reaction

    e.   acid-base neutralization reaction

Answer:

    c.   In the reaction, Pb and K exchange their anions in a double-displacement reaction.

2. An example of a balanced equation is

    a. $KClO_3 \rightarrow KCl + 3O_2$

    b. $2KClO_3 \rightarrow KCl + 2O_2$

    c. $2KClO_3 \rightarrow 2KCl + 3O_2$

    d. $4KClO_3 \rightarrow 2KCl + 2O_2$

    e. $6KClO_3 \rightarrow 6KCl + 3O_2$

Answer:

    c.   In this equation, there are equal numbers of each type of atom on both sides (two K atoms, two Cl atoms, and six O atoms).

Mixtures

When substances are combined without a chemical reaction to bond them, the resulting substance is called a **mixture**. Physical changes can be used to separate mixtures. For example, heating salt water until the water evaporates, leaving the salt behind, will separate a salt water solution.

In a mixture, the components can be unevenly distributed, such as in trail mix or soil. These mixtures are described at **heterogeneous**. Alternatively, the components can be **homogeneously**, or uniformly, distributed, as in salt water.

A **solution** is a special type of stable homogeneous mixture. The components of a solution will not separate on their own and cannot be separated using a filter. The substance being dissolved is the **solute**, and the substance acting on the solute, or doing the dissolving, is the **solvent**.

> Did You Know? Solutions can exist as solids, liquids, or gases. For example, carbonated water has a gaseous solute (CO_2) and a liquid solvent (water). A solution formed by combining two solid metals, such as stainless steel, is an **alloy**.

The **solubility** of a solution is the maximum amount of solute that will dissolve in a specific quantity of solvent at a specified temperature. Solutions can be saturated, unsaturated, or supersaturated based on the amount of solute dissolved in the solution.

+ A **saturated** solution has the maximum amount of solute that can be dissolved in the solvent.

+ An **unsaturated** solution contains less solute than a saturated solution would hold.

+ A **supersaturated solution** contains more solvent than a saturated solution. A supersaturated solution can be made by heating the solution to dissolve additional solute and then slowly cooling it down to a specified temperature.

PRACTICE QUESTIONS

1. A heterogeneous mixture is one in which

   a. the atoms or molecules are distributed unevenly

   b. two substances are in different states

   c. there is a mixture of covalent and ionic compounds

   d. there is a mixture of polar and nonpolar molecules

   e. three or more different molecules are mixed together

   Answer:

   a. A heterogeneous mixture is any nonuniform mixture, which means the atoms or molecules are unevenly distributed.

2. A solution in which more solvent can be dissolved is called

   a. unsaturated

   b. saturated

   c. supersaturated

   d. homogeneous

   e. heterogeneous

Answer:

a. An unsaturated solution has less solute than can be dissolved in the given amount of solvent.

Acids and Bases

Acids and bases are substances that share a distinct set of physical properties. **Acids** are corrosive, sour, and change the color of vegetable dyes like litmus from blue to red. **Bases**, or alkaline solutions, are slippery, bitter, and change the color of litmus from red to blue.

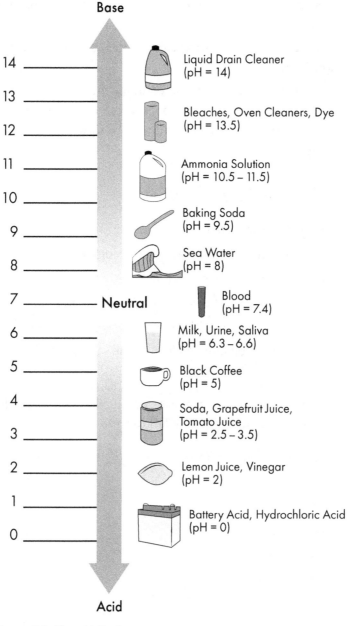

Figure 7.6. The pH Scale

There are a number of different ways to define acids and bases, but generally acids release hydrogen ions (H^+) in solution, while bases release hydroxide (OH^-) ions. For example, hydrochloric acid (HCl) ionizes, or breaks apart, in solution to release H^+ ions:

$$HCl \rightarrow H^+ + Cl$$

The base sodium hydroxide (NaOH) ionizes to release OH^- ions:

$$NaOH \rightarrow Na^+ + OH^-$$

Acids and bases combine in a **neutralization reaction**. During the reaction, the H^+ and OH^- ions join to form water, and the remaining ions combine to form a salt:

$$HCl + NaOH \rightarrow H_2O + NaCl$$

Did You Know? A **buffer**, or buffer solution, is a solution that resists changes in pH when small quantities of acids or bases are added. A buffer can do this because it contains a weak acid to react with any added base and a weak base to react with any added acid.

The strength of an acid or base is measured on the **pH scale**, which ranges from 1 to 14, with 1 being the strongest acid, 14 being the strongest base, and 7 being neutral. A substance's pH value is a measure of how many hydrogen ions are in the solution. The scale is logarithmic, meaning an acid with a pH of 3 has ten times as many hydrogen ions as an acid with a pH of 4. Water, which separates into equal numbers of H^+ and OH^- ions, has a neutral pH of 7.

PRACTICE QUESTIONS

1. A neutralization reaction produces

    a. a base

    b. a buffer

    c. hydrogen ions

    d. a salt

    e. an acid

    Answer:

    d. A neutralization reaction occurs when an acid and a base combine to form a salt and water.

2. When a nitric acid solution is diluted by a factor of ten, the pH will

    a. go up ten units

    b. go down ten units

    c. go up one unit

    d. go down one unit

    e. stay the same

c. The pH will go up: diluting an acid will decrease the concentration of H⁺ ions, and higher pH values represent lower concentrations of H⁺ ions. Diluting the acid by a factor of ten will change the pH one unit because the pH scale is logarithmic.

Motion

To study motion, it is necessary to understand the concept of scalars and vectors. **Scalars** are measurements that have a quantity but no direction. **Vectors**, in contrast, have both a quantity and a direction. **Distance** is a scalar: it describes how far an object has traveled along a path. Distance can have values such as 54 m or 16 miles. **Displacement** is a vector: it describes how far an object has traveled from its starting position. A displacement value will indicate direction, such as 54 m east or –16 miles.

Table 7.4. Physical Science Units

mass	kilograms (kg)
displacement	meters (m)
velocity	meters per second (m/s)
acceleration	meters per second per second (m/s²)
force	Newtons (N)
work	Joules (J)
energy	Joules (J)
current	amperes (A)
voltage	volts (V)

Speed describes how quickly something is moving. It is found by dividing distance by time, and so is a scalar value. **Velocity** is the rate at which an object changes position. Velocity is found by dividing displacement by time, meaning it is a vector value. An object that travels a certain distance and then returns to its starting point has a velocity of zero because its final position did not change. Its speed, however, can be found by dividing the total distance it traveled by the time it took to make the trip.

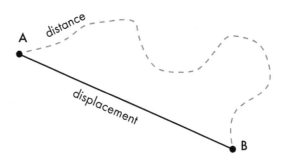

Figure 7.7. Distance versus Displacement

Acceleration describes how quickly an object changes velocity. It is also a vector: when acceleration is in the same direction as velocity, the object will move faster. When the acceleration is in the opposite direction of velocity, the object will slow down.

PRACTICE QUESTION

A person who starts from rest and increases his velocity to 5 m/s over a time period of 1 second has an acceleration of

a. -5 m/s^2

b. 0 m/s^2

c. 1 m/s^2

d. 5 m/s^2

e. 10 m/s^2

Answer:

d.   Acceleration is the change in velocity over the change in time:

$$a = \frac{v}{t} = \frac{(5 \text{ m/s} - 0 \text{ m/s})}{1 \text{ s}} = \textbf{5 m/s}^2$$

Forces

A push or pull that causes an object to move or change direction is called a **force**. Forces can arise from a number of different sources.

+   **Gravity** is the attraction of one mass to another mass. For example, the earth's gravitational field pulls objects toward it, and the sun's gravitational field keeps planets in motion around it.

+   **Electrical force** is the creation of a field by charged particles that will cause other charged objects in that field to move.

+   **Tension** is found in ropes pulling or holding up an object.

+   **Friction** is created by two objects moving against each other.

+   **Normal force** occurs when an object is resting on another object.

+   **Buoyant force** is the upward force experienced by floating objects.

In 1687, Isaac Newton published **three laws of motion** that describe the behavior of force and mass. Newton's first law is also called the **law of inertia**. It states that an object will maintain its current state of motion unless acted on by an outside force.

Newton's **second law** is an equation, $F = ma$. The equation states that increasing the force on an object will increase its acceleration. In addition, the mass of the object will determine its acceleration: under the same force, a small object will accelerate more quickly than a larger object.

An object in equilibrium is either at rest or is moving at constant velocity; in other words, the object has no acceleration, or $a = 0$. Using Newton's second law, an object is in equilibrium if the net force on the object is 0, or $F = 0$ (this is called the equilibrium condition).

Newton's **third law** states that for every action (force), there will be an equal and opposite reaction (force). For instance, if a person is standing on the floor, there is a force of gravity pulling him toward the earth. However, he is not accelerating toward the earth; he is simply standing at rest on the floor (in equilibrium). So, the floor must provide a force that is equal in magnitude and in the opposite direction to the force of gravity.

PRACTICE QUESTIONS

1. A book resting on a table is prevented from falling on the floor by

    a. gravity

    b. tension

    c. friction

    d. electromagnetic force

    e. normal force

    Answer:

    e. The normal force pushes up to counterbalance the force of gravity, which points down.

2. An example of an object in equilibrium is

    a. a parachutist after he jumps from an airplane

    b. an airplane taking off

    c. a person sitting still in a chair

    d. a soccer ball when it is kicked

    e. the moon orbiting the earth

    Answer:

    c. A person sitting in a chair is not accelerating. All the other choices describe objects that are accelerating or changing velocity.

Work

Work is a scalar value that is defined as the application of a force over a distance. It is measured in Joules (J).

A person lifting a book off the ground is an example of someone doing work. The book has a weight because it is being pulled toward the earth. As the person lifts the book, her hand and arm are producing a force that is larger than that weight, causing the book to rise. The higher the person lifts the book, the more work is done.

The sign of the work done is important. In the example of lifting a book, the person's hand is doing positive (+) work on the book. However, gravity is always pulling the book down, which means that during a lift, gravity is doing negative (−) work on the book. If the force and the displacement are in the same direction, then the work is positive (+). If the force and the displacement are in opposite directions, then the work is negative (−). In the case of lifting a book, the net work done on the book is positive.

PRACTICE QUESTION

The most work is done on a car when

a.   pushing on the car, but it does not move

b.   towing the car up a steep hill for 100 m

c.   pushing the car 5 m across a parking lot

d.   painting the car

e.   driving the car in reverse for 5 m

Answer:

b.   A steep hill requires a large force to counter the gravitational force. The large distance will also lead to a large amount of work done. Less work is done in choices c and e, and no work is done in choice a. Choice d is incorrect because painting the car is "work," but not the technical definition of work. The car is not moving while being painted, so no work is done on the car.

Energy

Energy is an abstract concept, but everything in nature has an energy associated with it. Energy is measured in Joules (J). There are many types of energy:

+ mechanical: the energy of motion
+ chemical: the energy in chemical bonds
+ thermal: the energy of an object due to its temperature
+ nuclear: the energy in the nucleus of an atom
+ electric: the energy arising from charged particles
+ magnetic: the energy arising from a magnetic field

There is an energy related to movement called the **kinetic energy (KE)**. Any object that has mass and is moving will have a kinetic energy.

Potential energy (PE) is the energy stored in a system; it can be understood as the potential for an object to gain kinetic energy. There are several types of potential energy.

+ **Electric potential energy** is derived from the interaction between positive and negative charges.
+ Compressing a spring stores **elastic potential energy.**

- ✦ Energy is also stored in chemical bonds as **chemical potential energy.**
- ✦ The energy stored by objects due to their height is **gravitational potential energy.**

Energy can be converted into other forms of energy, but it cannot be created or destroyed. This principle is called the **conservation of energy.** A swing provides a simple example of this principle. Throughout the swing's path, the total energy of the system remains the same. At the highest point of a swing's path, it has potential energy but no kinetic energy (because it has stopped moving momentarily as it changes direction). As the swing drops, that potential energy is converted to kinetic energy, and the swing's velocity increases. At the bottom of its path, all its potential energy has been converted into kinetic energy (meaning its potential energy is zero). This process repeats as the swing moves up and down. At any point in the swing's path, the kinetic and potential energies will sum to the same value.

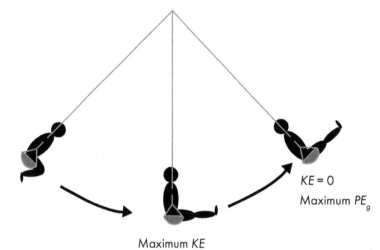

Figure 7.8. Conservation of Energy in a Swing

PRACTICE QUESTION

The energy stored in a compressed spring is

a.   nuclear energy

b.   mechanical energy

c.   chemical potential energy

d.   gravitational potential energy

e.   elastic potential energy

Answer:

e.   Compressing a spring stores elastic potential energy, which is turned into kinetic energy when the spring is released.

Waves

Energy can also be transferred through **waves**, which are repeating pulses of energy. Waves that travel through a medium, like ripples on a pond or compressions in a Slinky, are called **mechanical waves**. Waves that vibrate up and down (like the ripples on a pond) are **transverse waves**, and those that travel through compression (like the Slinky) are **longitudinal waves**. Mechanical waves will travel faster through denser mediums; for example, sound waves will move faster through water than through air.

Longitudinal Wave

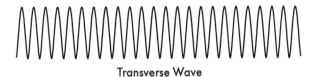

Transverse Wave

Figure 7.9. Types of Waves

Waves can be described using a number of different properties. A wave's highest point is called its **crest**, and its lowest point is the **trough**. A wave's **midline** is halfway between the crest and trough; the **amplitude** describes the distance between the midline and the crest (or trough). The distance between crests (or troughs) is the **wavelength**. A wave's **period** is the time it takes for a wave to go through one complete cycle, and the number of cycles a wave goes through in a specific period of time is its **frequency**.

Sound is a special type of longitudinal wave created by vibrations. Our ears are able to interpret these waves as particular sounds. The frequency, or rate, of the vibration determines the sound's **pitch**. **Loudness** depends on the amplitude, or height, of a sound wave.

The **Doppler effect** is the difference in perceived pitch caused by the motion of the object creating the wave. For example, as an ambulance approaches an observer, the siren's pitch will appear to increase, and then as the ambulance moves away, the siren's pitch will appear to decrease. This occurs because sound waves are compressed as the ambulance approaches the observer and are spread out as the ambulance moves away from the observer.

Electromagnetic waves are composed of oscillating electric and magnetic fields and thus do not require a medium through which to travel. The electromagnetic spectrum classifies the types of electromagnetic waves based on their frequency. These include radio waves, microwaves, X-rays, and visible light.

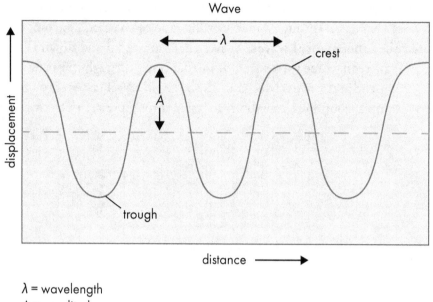

λ = wavelength
A = amplitude

Figure 7.10. Parts of a Wave

The study of light is called **optics**. Because visible light is a wave, it will display properties that are similar to other waves. It will **reflect**, or bounce off, surfaces, which can be observed by shining a flashlight on a mirror. Light will also **refract**, or bend, when it travels between substances. This effect can be seen by placing a pencil in water and observing the apparent bend in the pencil.

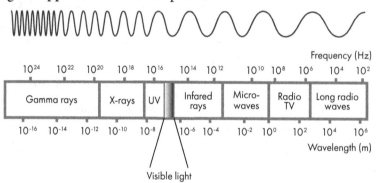

Figure 7.11. The Electromagnetic Spectrum

Curved pieces of glass called **lenses** can be used to bend light in a way that affects how an image is perceived. Some microscopes, for example, make objects appear larger through the use of specific types of lenses. Eyeglasses also use lenses to correct poor vision.

The frequency of a light wave is responsible for its color, with red/orange colors having a lower frequency than blue/violet colors. White light is a blend of all the frequencies of visible light. Passing white light through a prism will bend each frequency at a slightly different angle, separating the colors and creating a rainbow. Sunlight passing through raindrops can undergo this effect, creating large rainbows in the sky.

PRACTICE QUESTION

Refraction, the bending of waves, can cause

a. rainbows

b. echoes

c. loudness

d. reflections in mirrors

e. the Doppler effect

Answer:

a. Rainbows are created when light passes through an object, such as a raindrop or prism, that causes the colors in light to bend at different angles.

Electricity and Magnetism

Electric charge is created by a difference in the balance of protons and electrons, which creates a positively or negatively charged object. Charged objects create an **electric field** that spreads outward from the object. Other charged objects in that field will experience a force: objects that have opposite charges will be attracted to each other, and objects with the same charge will be repelled, or pushed away, from each other.

Because protons cannot leave the nucleus, charge is created by the movement of electrons. **Static electricity**, or electrostatic charge, occurs when a surface has a buildup of charges. For example, if a student rubs a balloon on her head, the friction will cause electrons to move from her hair to the balloon. This creates a negative charge on the balloon and a positive charge on her hair; the resulting attraction will cause her hair to move toward the balloon.

Electricity is the movement of electrons through a conductor, and an electric circuit is a closed loop through which electricity moves. Circuits include a **voltage** source, which powers the movement of electrons known as **current**. Sources of voltage include batteries, generators, and wall outlets (which are in turn powered by electric power stations). Other elements, such as lights, computers, and microwaves, can then be connected to the circuit and then powered by its electricity.

Magnets are created by the alignment of spinning electrons within a substance. This alignment will occur naturally in some substances, including iron, nickel, and cobalt, all of which can be used to produce permanent magnets. The alignment of electrons creates a magnetic field, which, like an electric or gravitational field, can act on other objects. Magnetic fields have a north and a south pole that act similarly to electric charges: opposite poles will attract, and same poles will repel each other. However, unlike electric charge, which can be either positive or negative, a magnetic field ALWAYS has two poles. If a magnet is cut in half, the result is two magnets, each with a north and a south pole.

Electricity and magnetism are closely related. A moving magnet creates an electric field, and a moving charged particle creates a magnetic field. A specific kind of temporary magnet known as an **electromagnet** can be made by coiling a wire around a metal object and running electricity through it. A magnetic field will be created when the wire contains a current but will disappear when the flow of electricity is stopped.

PRACTICE QUESTION

The particles that flow through a circuit to power a light bulb are

a.   protons

b.   neutrons

c.   electrons

d.   nucleus

e.   atoms

Answer:

c.   Electrons are negatively charged subatomic particles that exist outside the nucleus of an atom. A power source forces moving electrons through a circuit.

Test Your Knowledge

Read the question, and then choose the most correct answer.

1. Which of the following determines the atomic number of an atom?

   a. the number of electrons orbiting the nucleus

   b. the number of protons in the nucleus

   c. the number of protons and neutrons in the nucleus

   d. the number of protons and electrons in the atom

2. How many neutrons are in an atom of the element $^{88}_{38}Sr$?

   a. 38

   b. 88

   c. 50

   d. 126

3. Refer to the periodic table in Figure 7.2. Which element is a metalloid?

   a. rubidium

   b. vanadium

   c. antimony

   d. iodine

4. Which of the following is NOT a typical property of metals?

   a. Metals have low densities.

   b. Metals are malleable.

   c. Metals are good conductors of electricity and heat.

   d. Metals in solid state consist of ordered structures with tightly packed atoms.

5. Which element has chemical properties most similar to sulfur?

   a. fluorine

   b. argon

   c. phosphorus

   d. oxygen

6. Which of the following groups on the periodic table will typically adopt a charge of +1 when forming ionic compounds?

   a. alkaline earth metals

   b. lanthanides

   c. actinides

   d. alkali metals

7. Match the elements with the type of bond that would occur between them.

Elements	Bond
magnesium and bromine	
carbon and oxygen	
solid copper	

   a. ionic

   b. metallic

   c. covalent

8. Label each compound as polar or nonpolar.

Compound	Polar	Nonpolar
H_2O		
F_2		
HF		

9. How many electrons are included in the double bond between the two oxygen atoms in O_2?

a. 2
b. 4
c. 6
d. 8

10. Which of the following describes a physical change?

a. Water becomes ice.
b. Batter is baked into a cake.
c. An iron fence rusts.
d. A firecracker explodes.

11. Which of the following processes produces a gas from a solid?

a. melting
b. evaporation
c. condensation
d. sublimation

12. Which of the following is a double-replacement reaction?

a. HNO_3 (aq) + NaOH (aq) → $NaNO_3$ (aq) + H_2O (l)
b. CS_2 (g) + CO_2 (g) → 2COS (g)
c. $2N_2O$ (g) → $2N_2$ (g) + O_2 (g)
d. $BaCl_2$ (aq) + H_2SO_4 (aq) → 2HCl (aq) + $BaSO_4$ (s)

13. Balance the following chemical equation:

$P_4 + O_2 + H_2O → H_3PO_4$

a. 1:8:6:4
b. 1:2:2:4
c. 1:2:6:4
d. 1:5:6:4

14. Which of the following is NOT a homogeneous mixture?

a. air
b. sandy water
c. brass
d. salt dissolved in water

15. Which trait defines a saturated solution?

a. Both the solute and solvent are liquid.
b. The solute is distributed evenly throughout the solution.
c. The solute is unevenly distributed throughout the solution.
d. No more solute can be dissolved in the solution.

16. Which of the following is NOT a definition of an acid?

a. A substance that contains hydrogen and produces H^+ in water.
b. A substance that donates protons to a base.
c. A substance that reacts with a base to form a salt and water.
d. A substance that accepts protons.

17. A ball is tossed straight into the air with a velocity of 3 m/s. What will its velocity be at its maximum height?

a. −3 m/s
b. 0 m/s
c. 1.5 m/s
d. 3 m/s

18. How far will a car moving at 40 m/s travel in 2 seconds?

a. 10 m
b. 20 m
c. 40 m
d. 80 m

19. If a baseball thrown straight up in the air takes 5 seconds to reach its peak, how long will it need to fall back to the player's hand?

    a.   2.5 seconds

    b.   9.8 seconds

    c.   5.0 seconds

    d.   10.0 seconds

20. Which of the following is a measure of the inertia of an object?

    a.   mass

    b.   speed

    c.   acceleration

    d.   force

21. A box sliding down a ramp experiences all of the following forces EXCEPT

    a.   tension.

    b.   friction.

    c.   gravitational.

    d.   normal.

22. A person with a mass of 80 kg travels to the moon, where the acceleration due to gravity is 1.62 m/s^2. What will her mass be on the moon?

    a.   greater than 80 kg

    b.   80 kg

    c.   less than 80 kg

    d.   The answer cannot be determined without more information.

23. If a force of 300 N is pushing on a block to the right and a force of 400 N is pushing on a block to the left, what is the net force on the block?

    a.   0 N

    b.   100 N to the left

    c.   300 N to the right

    d.   400 N to the left

24. A man is pushing against a heavy rock sitting on a flat plane, and the rock is not moving. The force that holds the rock in place is

    a.   friction.

    b.   gravity.

    c.   normal force.

    d.   buoyant force.

25. Which of the following describes what will happen when positive work is done on an object?

    a.   The object will gain energy.

    b.   The object will lose energy.

    c.   The object will increase its temperature.

    d.   The object will decrease its temperature.

26. What type of energy is stored in the bond between hydrogen and oxygen in water (H_2O)?

    a.   mechanical

    b.   chemical

    c.   nuclear

    d.   electric

27. A microscope makes use of which property of waves to make objects appear larger?

    a.   diffraction

    b.   amplitude

    c.   reflection

    d.   refraction

28. Which measurement describes the distance between crests in a wave?

    a.   amplitude

    b.   wavelength

    c.   frequency

    d.   period

29. Two negative charges are being held 1 meter apart. What will the charges do when they are released?

a. They will move closer together.

b. They will move farther apart.

c. They will stay 1 meter apart and move in the same direction.

d. They will stay 1 meter apart and not move.

30. The north poles of two magnets are held near each other. At which distance will the magnets experience the most force?

a. 0.1 meters

b. 1 meters

c. 10 meters

d. 100 meters

ANSWER KEY

1. b.

Atomic number is defined as the total number of protons in the nucleus of an atom.

2. c.

Subtracting the atomic number from the mass number gives the number of protons: $A - Z = 88 - 38 = 50$.

3. c.

Antimony is a metalloid. Rubidium is a metal, vanadium is a transition metal, and iodine is a halogen.

4. a.

Because metals tend to consist of ordered, tightly packed atoms, their densities are typically high (not low).

5. d.

Oxygen is in the same group as sulfur and is also a nonmetal.

6. d.

By losing one electron and thereby adopting a +1 charge, alkali metals achieve a noble gas electron configuration, making them more stable.

7.

Elements	Bond
magnesium and bromine	a. is correct. Ionic bonds form between elements on the left side of the periodic table and the right side.
carbon and oxygen	c. is correct. Nonmetals tend to form covalent bonds.
solid copper	b. is correct. Solid metals are held together by metallic bonding.

8.

Compound	Polar	Nonpolar
H_2O	O attracts electrons more strongly than H, and H_2O is bent such that the charges on each O do not balance.	
F_2		Because the two atoms are the same, they share electrons equally.
HF	F attracts electrons more strongly than H, creating a polar molecule.	

9. b.

The two oxygen atoms in a covalent double bond share two pairs of electrons, or four total.

10. a.

When water changes form, it does not change the chemical composition of the substance. Once water becomes ice, the ice can easily turn back into water.

11. d.

Sublimation is the phase change in which a material moves directly from the solid phase to the gas phase, bypassing the liquid phase.

12. d.

This reaction is a double-replacement reaction in which the two reactants change partners. Ba^{+2} combines with SO_4^{-2} and H^{+1} combines with Cl^{-1}.

13. d.

$$\_P_4 + \_O_2 + \_H_2O \rightarrow \_H_3PO_4$$

Add a 4 on the right side to balance the four P atoms on the left.

$$\_P_4 + \_O_2 + \_H_2O \rightarrow 4H_3PO_4$$

There are now twelve H atoms on the right, so add a 6 to H_2O on the left.

$$\_P_4 + \_O_2 + 6H_2O \rightarrow 4H_3PO_4$$

There are sixteen O on the right, so add a 5 to O_2 on the left.

$$P_4 + 5O_2 + 6H_2O \rightarrow 4H_3PO_4$$

14. b.

Sandy water is not a homogeneous mixture. Sand and water can be easily separated, making it a heterogeneous mixture.

15. d.

No more solute can be dissolved into a saturated solution.

16. d.

Acids increase the concentration of hydrogen ions in solution and do not accept protons.

17. b.

The velocity of a projectile is zero at its maximum height.

18. d.

Displacement is equal to velocity multiplied by time:

$$d = vt = (40 \text{ m/s})(2 \text{ s}) = 80 \text{ m}$$

19. c.

The time to the peak and the time to fall back to the original height are equal.

20. a.

Mass is a measure of an object's inertia.

21. a.

Tension is the force that results from objects being pulled or hung.

22. b.

The mass of an object is constant, so the mass would still be 80 kg. (However, the person's weight would be lower on the moon than on the earth.)

23. b.

The total force on an object is found by adding all the individual forces: 300 N + (−400 N) = −100 N (where negative is to the left).

24. a.

When the man pushes on the rock, static friction points opposite the direction of the applied force with the same magnitude. The forces add to zero, so the rock's acceleration is also zero.

25. a.

The object will gain energy.

26. b.

Chemical energy is stored in the bonds between atoms.

27. d.

Lenses refract, or bend, light waves to make objects appear larger.

28. b.

Wavelength is the length of each cycle of the wave, which can be found by measuring between crests.

29. b.

Like charges repel each other, so the two charges will move apart from each other.

30. a.

Magnetic force is inversely proportional to the distance between two objects, so the smallest distance will create the largest force.

EIGHT: EARTH AND SPACE SCIENCE

Astronomy

Astronomy is the study of space. Our planet, **Earth**, is just one out of a group of planets that orbit the sun, which is the star at the center of our solar system. Other planets in our solar system include Mercury, Venus, Mars, Jupiter, Saturn, Uranus, and Neptune. Every planet, except Mercury and Venus, has **moons**, or naturally occurring satellites that orbit a planet. Our solar system also includes **asteroids** and **comets**, small rocky or icy objects that orbit the Sun. Many of these are clustered in the **asteroid belt**, which is located between the orbits of Mars and Jupiter.

Figure 8.1. Solar System

Our solar system is a small part of a bigger star system called a **galaxy**. (Our galaxy is called the Milky Way.) Galaxies consist of stars, gas, and dust held together by gravity and contain millions of **stars**, which are hot balls of plasma and gases. The universe includes many types of stars, including supergiant stars, white dwarfs, giant stars, and neutron stars. Stars form in **nebulas**, which are large clouds of dust and gas. When very large stars collapse, they create **black holes**, which have a gravitational force so strong that light cannot escape.

Earth, the moon, and the sun interact in a number of ways that impact life on our planet. When the positions of the three align, eclipses occur. A **lunar eclipse** occurs when Earth lines up between the moon and the sun; the moon moves into the shadow of Earth and appears dark in color. A **solar eclipse** occurs when the moon lines up between Earth and the sun; the moon covers the sun, blocking sunlight.

The cycle of day and night and the seasonal cycle are determined by the earth's motion. It takes approximately 365 days, or one **year**, for Earth to revolve around the sun. While Earth is revolving around the sun, it is also rotating on its axis, which takes approximately twenty-four hours, or one **day**. As the planet rotates, different areas alternately face toward the sun and away from the sun, creating night and day.

The earth's axis is not directly perpendicular to its orbit, meaning the planet tilts on its axis. The **seasons** are caused by this tilt. When the Northern Hemisphere is tilted toward the sun, it receives more sunlight and experiences summer. At the same time that the Northern Hemisphere experiences summer, the Southern Hemisphere, which receives less direct sunlight, experiences winter. As the earth revolves, the Northern Hemisphere will tilt away from the sun and move into winter, while the Southern Hemisphere tilts toward the sun and moves into summer.

PRACTICE QUESTION

The phenomenon that occurs when the moon moves between the earth and the sun is called a(n)

a.   aurora

b.   lunar eclipse

c.   black hole

d.   solar eclipse

e.   solstice

Answer:

d.   When the moon moves between the earth and the sun, a solar eclipse occurs, blocking sunlight from the planet.

Geology

Geology is the study of the minerals and rocks that make up the earth. A **mineral** is a naturally occurring, solid, inorganic substance with a crystalline structure. There are several properties that help identify a mineral, including color, luster, hardness, and density. Examples of minerals include talc, diamonds, and topaz.

> 🔍 Did You Know? Luster describes how light reflects off the surface of a mineral. Terms to describe luster include dull, metallic, pearly, and waxy.

Although a **rock** is also a naturally occurring solid, it can be either organic or inorganic and is composed of one or more minerals. Rocks are classified based on their method of formation. The three types of rocks are igneous, sedimentary, and metamorphic. **Igneous rocks** are the result of tectonic processes that bring magma, or melted rock, to the earth's surface; they can form either above or below the surface. **Sedimentary rocks** are formed from the compaction of rock fragments that results from weathering and erosion. Lastly, **metamorphic rocks** form when extreme temperature and pressure cause the structure of pre-existing rocks to change.

The **rock cycle** describes how rocks form and break down. Typically, the cooling and solidification of magma as it rises to the surface creates igneous rocks. These rocks are then subject to **weathering**, the mechanical and/or chemical processes by which rocks break down. During **erosion** the resulting sediment is deposited in a new location. As sediment is deposited, the resulting compaction creates new sedimentary rocks. As new layers are added, rocks and minerals are forced closer to the earth's core where they are subjected to heat and pressure, resulting in metamorphic rock. Eventually, they will

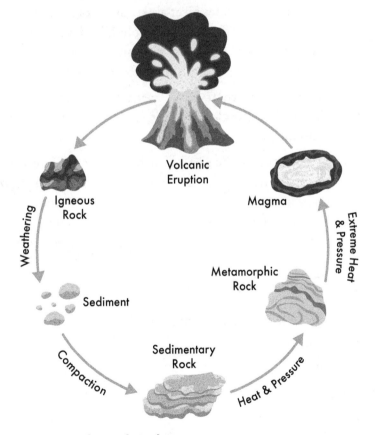

Figure 8.2. The Rock Cycle

reach their melting point and return to magma, starting the cycle over again. This process takes place over hundreds of thousands or even millions of years.

Paleontology, the study of the history of life on Earth, is sometimes also considered part of geology. Paleontologists study the rock record, which retains biological history through **fossils**, the preserved remains and traces of ancient life. Fossils can be used to learn about the evolution of life on the planet, particularly bacteria, plants, and animals that have gone extinct. Throughout Earth's history, there have been five documented catastrophic events that caused major extinctions. For each mass extinction, there are several theories about the cause but no definitive answers. Theories about what triggered mass extinctions include climate change, ice ages, asteroid and comet impacts, and volcanic activity.

The surface of the earth is made of large plates that float on the less dense layer beneath them. These **tectonic plates** make up the lithosphere, the planet's surface layer. Over 200 million years ago, the continents were joined together in one giant landmass called **Pangea**. Due to **continental drift**, or the slow movement of tectonic plates, the continents gradually shifted to their current positions.

> Helpful Hint: The magnitude of an earthquake refers to the amount of energy it releases, measured as the maximum motion during the earthquake. This can indirectly describe how destructive the earthquake was.

The boundaries where plates meet are the locations for many geologic features and events. **Mountains** are formed when plates collide and push land upward, and **trenches** form when one plate is pushed beneath another. In addition, the friction created by plates sliding past each other is responsible for most **earthquakes**.

Volcanoes, which are vents in the earth's crust that allow molten rock to reach the surface, frequently occur along the edges of tectonic plates. However, they can also occur at hotspots located far from plate boundaries.

The outermost layer of the earth, which includes tectonic plates, is called the **lithosphere**. Beneath the lithosphere are, in order, the **asthenosphere**, **mesosphere**, and **core**. The core includes two parts: the **outer core** is a liquid layer, and the **inner core** is composed of solid iron. It is believed the inner core spins at a rate slightly different from the rest of the planet, which creates the earth's magnetic field.

PRACTICE QUESTION

Rocks are broken down through the process of

a. fossilization

b. compaction

c. sedimentation

d. erosion

e. weathering

e. Weathering is the process in which rocks are broken down into smaller pieces by physical or chemical means.

Hydrology

The earth's surface includes many bodies of water that together form the **hydrosphere**. The largest of these are the bodies of salt water called **oceans**. There are five oceans: the Arctic, Atlantic, Indian, Pacific, and Southern. Together, the oceans account for 71 percent of the earth's surface and 97 percent of the earth's water.

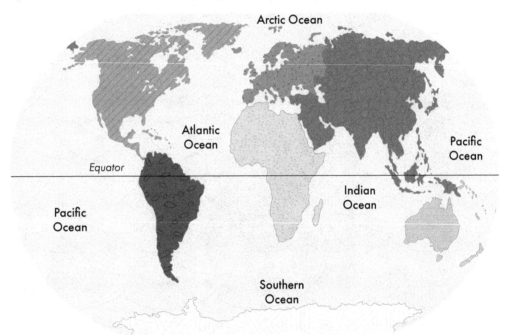

Figure 8.3. The Earth's Oceans

Oceans are subject to cyclic rising and falling water levels at shorelines called **tides**, which are the result of the gravitational pull of the moon and sun. The oceans also experience **waves**, which are caused by the movement of energy through the water.

Other bodies of water include **lakes**, which are usually freshwater, and **seas**, which are usually saltwater. **Rivers** and streams are moving bodies of water that flow into lakes, seas, and oceans. The earth also contains groundwater, or water that is stored underground in rock formations called **aquifers**.

Much of the earth's water is stored as **ice**. The North and South Poles are usually covered in large sheets of ice called polar ice. **Glaciers** are large masses of ice and snow that move. Over long periods of time, they scour Earth's surface, creating features such as lakes and valleys. Large chunks of ice that break off from glaciers are called **icebergs**.

 Did You Know? 97 percent of the water on earth is saltwater. 68 percent of the remaining freshwater is locked up in ice caps and glaciers.

The **water cycle** is the circulation of water throughout the earth's surface, atmosphere, and hydrosphere. Water on the earth's surface evaporates, or changes from a liquid to a gas, and becomes water vapor. Plants also release water vapor through transpiration. Water vapor in the air then comes together to form clouds. When it cools, this water vapor condenses into a liquid and falls from the sky as precipitation, which includes rain, sleet, snow, and hail. Precipitation replenishes groundwater and the water found in features such as lakes and rivers, thus starting the cycle over again.

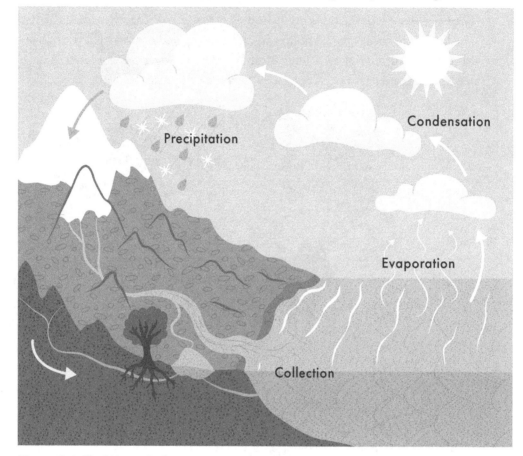

Figure 8.4. The Water Cycle

PRACTICE QUESTION

During the water cycle, groundwater is replenished by

a.   transpiration

b.   glaciers

c.   lakes

d.   precipitation

e.   evaporation

Answer:

d. Precipitation such as rain and snow seep into the ground to add to the groundwater supply.

Meteorology

Above the surface of Earth is the mass of gases called the **atmosphere**. The atmosphere includes the **troposphere**, which is closest to the earth, followed by the **stratosphere**, **mesosphere**, and **thermosphere**. The outermost layer of the atmosphere is the **exosphere**, which is located 6,200 miles above the surface. Generally, temperature in the atmosphere decreases with altitude. The **ozone layer**, which captures harmful radiation from the sun, is located in the stratosphere.

> Did You Know? Between each layer, a boundary exists where conditions change. This boundary takes the first part of the name of the previous layer followed by "pause." For example, the boundary between the troposphere and stratosphere is called the tropopause.

The **humidity**, or amount of water vapor in the air, and the **temperature** are two major atmospheric conditions that determine weather, the day-to-day changes in atmospheric conditions. A **warm front** occurs when warm air moves over a cold air mass, causing the air to feel warmer and more humid. A **cold front** occurs when cold air moves under a warm air mass, causing a drop in temperature.

Sometimes, weather turns violent. Tropical cyclones, or hurricanes, originate over warm ocean water. Hurricanes have destructive winds of more than 74 miles per hour and create large storm surges that can cause extensive damage along coastlines. Hurricanes, typhoons, and cyclones are all the same type of storm; they just have different names based on where the storm is located. **Hurricanes** originate in the Atlantic or Eastern Pacific Ocean, **typhoons** in the Western Pacific Ocean, and **cyclones** in the Indian Ocean. **Tornadoes** occur when unstable warm and cold air masses collide and a rotation is created by fast-moving winds.

The long-term weather conditions in a geographic location are called **climate**. A climate zone is a large area that experiences similar average temperature and precipitation. The three major climate zones, based on temperature, are the polar, temperate, and tropical zones. Each climate zone is subdivided into subclimates that have unique characteristics. The **tropical climate zone** (warm temperatures) can be subdivided into tropical wet, tropical wet and dry, semiarid, and arid. The **temperate climate zones** (moderate temperatures) include Mediterranean, humid subtropical, marine West Coast, humid continental, and subarctic. The **polar climate zones** (cold temperatures) include tundra, highlands, nonpermanent ice, and ice cap. Polar climates are cold and experience prolonged, dark winters due to the tilt of the earth's axis.

PRACTICE QUESTION

The layer of the atmosphere that absorbs harmful ultraviolet radiation from the sun is the

a. mesosphere

b. stratosphere

c. troposphere

d. thermosphere

e. exosphere

Answer:

b. The stratosphere contains a sublayer called the ozone layer, which absorbs harmful ultraviolet radiation from the sun.

Test Your Knowledge

Read the question, and then choose the most correct answer.

1. Which planet orbits closest to Earth?

    a. Mercury

    b. Venus

    c. Jupiter

    d. Saturn

2. What is the name of the phenomenon when a star suddenly increases in brightness and then disappears from view?

    a. aurora

    b. black hole

    c. eclipse

    d. supernova

3. How long does it take the earth to rotate on its axis?

    a. one hour

    b. one day

    c. one month

    d. one year

4. Which statement about the solar system is true?

    a. Earth is much closer to the sun than it is to other stars.

    b. The moon is closer to Venus than it is to Earth.

    c. At certain times of the year, Jupiter is closer to the sun than Earth is.

    d. Mercury is the closest planet to Earth.

5. When Earth moves between the moon and the sun, it is called a

    a. solar eclipse.

    b. lunar eclipse.

    c. black hole.

    d. supernova.

6. Which planet does not have a moon?

    a. Mercury

    b. Earth

    c. Jupiter

    d. Saturn

7. What is the term for the top layer of the earth's surface?

    a. lithosphere

    b. atmosphere

    c. biosphere

    d. asthenosphere

8. Which action is an example of mechanical weathering?

    a. Calcium carbonate reacts with water to form a cave.

    b. An iron gate rusts.

    c. Tree roots grow under the foundation of a house and cause cracks.

    d. Feldspar turns to clay when exposed to water.

9. Which of the following is caused by geothermal heat?

    a. geysers

    b. tsunamis

    c. tornadoes

    d. hurricanes

10. Which of the following holds the largest percentage of the earth's freshwater?

    a. glaciers and ice caps
    b. groundwater
    c. lakes
    d. oceans

11. Which of the following best describes how igneous rocks are formed?

    a. Sediment is compacted by pressure in the earth to form rock.
    b. Magma comes to the earth's surface and cools to form rock.
    c. Chemical weathering changes the composition of a rock to form new rock.
    d. Ancient plant and animal life is calcified to create rock.

12. Which of the following is true as altitude increases in the troposphere?

    a. Temperature and pressure increase.
    b. Temperature increases and pressure decreases.
    c. Temperature and pressure decrease.
    d. Temperature decreases and pressure increases.

13. Which statement about hurricanes and tornadoes is true?

    a. Hurricanes and tornadoes spin in opposite directions.
    b. Tornadoes do not occur in warm climates.
    c. Tornadoes have a low wind velocity.
    d. Hurricanes are formed over warm ocean water.

14. Which two properties are used to classify climate zones?

    a. latitude and temperature
    b. temperature and precipitation
    c. elevation and latitude
    d. precipitation and tilt of Earth's axis

15. Which of the following best describes continental drift?

    a. The mass extinction of the earth's species that occurred when a meteor struck the earth.
    b. The spinning of the earth's inner core that creates the earth's magnetic field.
    c. The formation of land masses from cooled magma.
    d. The movement of tectonic plates in the lithosphere.

CONTINUE

ANSWER KEY

1. b.

Venus's orbit is closest to Earth and is the second planet from the sun.

2. d.

Before a star collapses, the star burns brighter for a period of time and then fades from view. This is a supernova.

3. b.

Earth takes approximately twenty-four hours to rotate on its axis.

4. a.

The sun is about ninety-three million miles from Earth; the next closest star is about twenty-five trillion miles away.

5. b.

A lunar eclipse is when Earth moves between the moon and the sun.

6. a.

Only the first two planets, Mercury and Venus, lack moons.

7. a.

The lithosphere is the top layer of the earth's surface.

8. c.

Mechanical weathering involves breaking a substance down without changing the composition of the substance.

9. a.

Geysers are caused by geothermal heating of water underground.

10. a.

Glaciers and ice caps contain approximately 68.7% of all of Earth's freshwater supply, which is the largest percentage of the resources listed.

11. b.

Igneous rock is formed when magma (melted rock) is brought to the earth's surface and cools.

12. c.

Temperature and pressure both decrease with altitude in the troposphere.

13. d.

Hurricanes require warm ocean water to form.

14. b.

Climate zones are classified by temperature and precipitation.

15. d.

Continental drift is the movement of tectonic plates that lead to the current position of the continents.

NINE: VOCATIONAL ADJUSTMENT INDEX

The ninety questions on the Vocational Adjustment Index assess your personal attitudes, characteristics, and behaviors. Schools will use your score on this section to assess whether your personality is a fit for health care occupations.

Each question is a simple, general statement about personal or professional situations. You will choose to agree or disagree with the statement. You will need to work quickly to answer all the questions.

> **Vocational Adjustment Index Question Format**
>
> *The following statements address certain personal or professional situations. Agreeing or disagreeing with the statements simply reveals how you are likely to think, feel, or act in certain circumstances. If you agree with the statement, select (A) in the corresponding row. If you disagree, select (D). Choose the answer that is most true for you and answer immediately. Work rapidly.*
>
> 1. It is more important to be accurate than to be on time.   (A)   (D)
>
> 2. An ideal job includes a flexible schedule.   (A)   (D)
>
> 3. People who act like my friends have betrayed me.   (A)   (D)
>
> 4. It is difficult to make decisions in stressful situations.   (A)   (D)
>
> 5. Many people spend too much time on their phones.   (A)   (D)

There are no right or wrong answers, so there is no need to waste time deciding what the answer *should* be. Some statements are unflattering or critical, so it might be uncomfortable to select one. That is okay; it is best to answer as honestly as possible. You should also keep in mind that the chosen answers are not meant to be statements of fact. You don't have to select an answer that is necessarily a true statement about yourself, just the one that most generally applies to you.

TEN: Practice Test

ACADEMIC APTITUDE: VERBAL SKILLS

Which word is most different in meaning from the other words?

1.	a. distressed	b. worried	c. calm	d. anxious	e. stressed
2.	a. tired	b. exhausted	c. lazy	d. weary	e. energetic
3.	a. problem	b. complication	c. difficulty	d. certainty	e. obstacle
4.	a. mythical	b. ordinary	c. miraculous	d. magical	e. different
5.	a. rot	b. wither	c. thrive	d. fail	e. struggle
6.	a. attentive	b. thoughtless	c. responsible	d. caring	e. considerate
7.	a. complete	b. thorough	c. lacking	d. exhaustive	e. full
8.	a. laceration	b. scrape	c. bandage	d. wound	e. sore
9.	a. lively	b. dull	c. gloomy	d. somber	e. unhappy
10.	a. brief	b. terse	c. concise	d. long	e. sudden
11.	a. secretive	b. obscure	c. mysterious	d. cryptic	e. obvious
12.	a. gloomy	b. upbeat	c. irritable	d. glum	e. moody
13.	a. obsession	b. attraction	c. passion	d. interest	e. indifference
14.	a. pleasant	b. amiable	c. kindly	d. cheerful	e. rude
15.	a. combine	b. connect	c. join	d. divide	e. unite
16.	a. destroy	b. finish	c. create	d. shatter	e. ruin
17.	a. cascade	b. drip	c. torrent	d. flood	e. surge

18. a. calm   b. quiet   c. conflict   d. peace   e. order

19. a. limited   b. endless   c. eternal   d. lasting   e. constant

20. a. acquit   b. excuse   c. pardon   d. disapprove   e. absolve

21. a. arrogance   b. humility   c. vanity   d. narcissism   e. smugness

22. a. weak   b. defective   c. broken   d. flawed   e. perfect

23. a. humble   b. bashful   c. timid   d. conceited   e. modest

24. a. civil   b. polite   c. refined   d. crude   e. gracious

25. a. absurd   b. playful   c. foolish   d. silly   e. serious

ACADEMIC APTITUDE: ARITHMETIC

Work the problem, and then choose the correct answer.

26. Danika bought two packages of ground beef weighing 1.73 lb and 2.17 lb. What was the total weight of the two packages in pounds?

    a. 0.44   b. 1.25   c. 3.81   d. 3.9   e. 4.2

27. Morris went shopping with $80. He spent $24.17 at the hardware store and $32.87 on clothes. How much money did he have left?

    a. $22.96   b. $23.04   c. $42.96   d. $55.83   e. $57.04

28. What is the remainder when 397 is divided by 4?

    a. 0   b. 1   c. 2   d. 3   e. 4

29. A teacher has 50 notebooks to hand out to students. If she has 16 students in her class, and each student receives 2 notebooks, how many notebooks will she have left over?

    a. 2   b. 16   c. 18   d. 32   e. 34

30. Michael is making cupcakes. He plans to give $\frac{1}{2}$ of the cupcakes to a friend and $\frac{1}{3}$ of the cupcakes to his coworkers. If he makes 48 cupcakes, how many will he have left over?

    a. 8   b. 10   c. 12   d. 16   e. 24

31. Which of the following is closest in value to 129,113 + 34,602?

    a. 162,000   b. 163,000   c. 164,000   d. 165,000   e. 166,000

32. Students board a bus at 7:45 a.m. and arrive at school at 8:20 a.m. For how many minutes are the students on the bus?

    a. 30   b. 35   c. 45   d. 50   e. 65

33. Micah has invited 23 friends to his house and is having pizza for dinner. If each pizza feeds 4 people, how many pizzas should he order?

    a. 4   b. 5   c. 6   d. 7   e. 8

34. Out of 1,560 students at Ward Middle School, 15% want to take French. Which expression represents how many students want to take French?

    a. 1560 ÷ 15   b. 1560 × 15   c. 1560 × 1.51   d. 1560 ÷ 0.15   e. 1560 × 0.15

35. At the grocery store, apples cost $1.89 per pound and oranges cost $2.19 per pound. How much would it cost to purchase 2 lb of apples and 1.5 lb of oranges?

    a. $6.62   b. $7.07   c. $7.14   d. $7.22   e. $7.67

36. Which digit is in the hundredths place when 1.3208 is divided by 5.2?

a. 0   b. 4   c. 5   d. 8   e. 9

37. 17.38 − 19.26 + 14.2 =

a. 12.08   b. 12.32   c. 16.08   d. 16.22   e. 50.84

38. If a person reads 40 pages in 45 minutes, approximately how many minutes will it take her to read 265 pages?

a. 180   b. 202   c. 236   d. 265   e. 298

39. The recommended ratio of nurses to patients in a critical care unit is 1 to 4. How many nurses should be on duty if there are 20 patients in the unit?

a. 4   b. 5   c. 7   d. 8   e. 10

40. Jim is taking care of eight patients during his shift. So far it has taken him 25 minutes to see two patients. At this rate, how many minutes will it take Jim to check in on all eight patients?

a. 50   b. 60   c. 100   d. 120   e. 125

41. Juan is packing a shipment of three books weighing 0.8 lb, 0.49 lb, and 0.89 lb. The maximum weight for the shipping box is 2.5 lb. How much more weight will the box hold in pounds?

a. 0.32   b. 0.48   c. 1.61   d. 2.18   e. 4.68

42. The average rainfall in May for Austin, Texas, is 4.5 in. In July, the average rainfall is 1.67 in. How many more inches of rain fall on average in May than in July?

a. 1.22   b. 2.69   c. 2.83   d. 2.97   e. 6.17

43. If a $285.48 bill will be split evenly between six people, how much will each person pay?

a. $47.58   b. $49.88   c. $225.48   d. $885.46   e. $1,712.88

44. A bridge is 119.7 m long in the summer. In the winter, the metal contracts, and the bridge shrinks by 1.05 m. How many meters long is the bridge in winter?

a. 109.2   b. 118.2   c. 118.65   d. 120.75   e. 130.2

45. Angelica bought a roast weighing 3.2 lb. If the roast cost $25.44, how much did it cost per pound?

a. $5.95   b. $7.44   c. $7.95   d. $8.14   e. $22.24

46. A box of books weighs 6.3 lb. If there are 18 books in the box, how many pounds does each book weigh?

a. 0.35   b. 1.134   c. 3.5   d. 11.34   e. 35

47. Carlos spent $1.68 on bananas. If bananas cost 48 cents per pound, how many pounds of bananas did he buy?

a. 1.2   b. 2.06   c. 2.16   d. 3.5   e. 8.1

48. Sally has $127 in her checking. An automatic draft takes out $150 for her electric bill. What is her balance after the automatic draft?

a. −$277   b. −$123   c. −$23   d. $23   e. $123

49. Five numbers have an average of 16. If the first four numbers have a sum of 68, what is the fifth number?

a. 12   b. 16   c. 52   d. 68   e. 80

50. The recommended dosage of a particular medication is 4 mL per 50 lb of body weight. What is the recommended dosage in milliliters for a person who weighs 175 lb?

a. 14   b. 25   c. 28   d. 44   e. 140

ACADEMIC APTITUDE: NONVERBAL SKILLS

Which shape correctly completes the statement?

51. △ is to ▲ as ◇ is to ?

a. ▽ b. ◈ c. ◇ d. ▥ e. ◇

52. M is to ◁ as ◖ is to ?

a. △ b. ▽ c. ◗ d. ◁ e. ○

53. ⬡ is to ⬢ as △ is to ?

a. ● b. ▲ c. ■ d. ◆ e. ◀

54. ◔ is to ◕ as ◷ is to ?

a. ◐ b. ◑ c. ◔ d. ◖ e. ◔

55. 8 is to 8 as 8 is to ?

a. 8 b. 8 c. 8 d. 8 e. 8

56. ▷ is to ◹ as ◤ is to ?

a. ◺ b. ◀ c. ◹ d. ◿ e. ◿

57. ⠛ is to ⠤ as ⠿ is to ?

a. ⠿ b. ⠉ c. ⠿ d. ⠏ e. ⠤

58. ⊟ is to ⊟ as ⊟ is to ?

a. ⊟ b. ⊟ c. ⊟ d. ⊟ e. ⊟

59. ⫿⦀ is to ⦀⫿ as ⫿⫿ is to ?

a. ⦀⫿ b. ⫿⫿ c. ⦀⫿ d. ⫿⦀ e. ⦀⫿

60. ⊔ is to ⊔⊔ as ⊏ is to ?

a. F b. ⊏ c. ⊏ d. F e. ⊏

61. ◵ is to ◶ as ◷ is to ?

a. ◔ b. ◵ c. ◶ d. ◵ e. ◷

62. ⌐ is to ⎾ as ⌐ is to ?

a. ⊓ b. ⊓ c. ⊓ d. ⊓ e. ⊓

63. ▯▯ is to ⊞ as ◹ is to ?

a. ◺ b. ⊞ c. ◹ d. ⊞ e. ⊠

64. ╱ is to ⌒ as ⌐ is to ?

a. ⬠ b. ⊏ c. ⊂ d. ⊔ e. ⬠

65. ▲○/○▽ is to ▲○/●▽ as ▲○/●▽ is to ?

a. ▲○/●▽ b. ▲○/○▽ c. ▲○/○▽ d. ▲○/●▽ e. ▲○/○▽

66. ⬚ is to ⬚ as ⬚ is to ?

a. ⬚ b. ⬚ c. ⬚ d. ⬚ e. ⬚

67. ◇◈ is to ◈ as ◈◇ is to ?

a. ◈ b. ◈◆ c. ◈ d. ◈ e. ◇◈

68. (x) is to (x) as (x) is to ?

a. ⊕ b. (x) c. ⊕ d. (x) e. (x)

69. ¦¦¦ is to ¦¦¦ as ¦¦¦ is to ?

a. ¦¦¦ b. ¦¦¦ c. ¦¦¦ d. ¦¦¦ e. ¦¦¦

70. ✕ is to ✕ as ✕ is to ?

a. ✕ b. ✕ c. ✕ d. ✕ e. ✕

71. ▢ is to ⊏ as ⌐ is to ?

a. ⅂ b. ⌐ c. ⊒ d. ▎ e. ∪

72. (x) is to (x) as (x) is to ?

a. (x) b. (x) c. (x) d. (+) e. (x)

73. ▢ is to ▬ as ◿ is to ?

a. ◢ b. ◣ c. ◢ d. ▲ e. ◿

74. ▢ is to ▢ as ▢ is to ?

a. ▢ b. ▢ c. ▢ d. ▢ e. ▢

75. ⅃ is to ∟ as ˥ is to ?

a. ∟ b. ⌐ c. ⌐ d. ⅃ e. ˥

SPELLING

Choose the correct spelling of the word.

1. a. muscle   b. muscle   c. mucsel

2. a. hormoan   b. hormmone   c. hormone

3. a. seesure   b. seizure   c. seazure

4. a. facilitees b. facilitys   c. facilities

5. a. decrease   b. decreese   c. decreace

6. a. transfusion b. transfussion c. transfution

7. a. annatome   b. anatomy   c. annatomy

8. a. daignoses   b. diagnosis   c. diegnosis

9. a. equepment   b. equipmint   c. equipment

10. a. stomach   b. stomache   c. stomeche

11. a. athritis   b. arthritis   c. arthritise

12. a. overy   b. ovary   c. ovarry

13. a. surgical   b. surgicle   c. sergical

14. a. allerjy   b. alerrgy   c. allergy

15. a. inflammation b. enflamation c. inflamation

16. a. poisson   b. pioson   c. poison

17. a. atrophy   b. attrophy   c. atrophe

18. a. stierile   b. sterile   c. steerile

19. a. cellular   b. celullar   c. celluler

20. a. tisue   b. tissue   c. tissu

21. a. artifitial b. artificial   c. artifacial

22. a. immediet   b. immidiate   c. immediate

23. a. droplat   b. dropplet   c. droplet

24. a. symptom   b. symptome   c. simptom

25. a. eleminate b. elemenate   c. eliminate

26. a. adhear   b. adhere   c. adher

27.	a. inable	b. enable	c. ennable
28.	a. varyous	b. various	c. variouse
29.	a. secression	b. secresion	c. secretion
30.	a. traumma	b. traumme	c. trauma
31.	a. exsessive	b. excesive	c. excessive
32.	a. bacteria	b. bactieria	c. bactteria
33.	a. funngas	b. funngus	c. fungus
34.	a. monetor	b. monitor	c. moniter
35.	a. abration	b. abrassion	c. abrasion
36.	a. multipal	b. multipple	c. multiple
37.	a. tremor	b. tremer	c. tremour
38.	a. involvment	b. envolvement	c. involvement
39.	a. respiritory	b. resperitory	c. respiratory
40.	a. craneal	b. cranial	c. crannial
41.	a. dissease	b. diseasse	c. disease
42.	a. artery	b. arttery	c. arterie
43.	a. vaine	b. vein	c. veine
44.	a. cronic	b. chronic	c. chronick
45.	a. accute	b. acutte	c. acute

READING COMPREHENSION

Reading Comprehension tests your ability to understand what you have read. Read each passage carefully. Each question is followed by four possible answer choices. Answer each question based on the material contained in each passage.

The greatest changes in sensory, motor, and perceptual development happen in the first two years of life. When babies are first born, most of their senses operate like those of adults. For example, babies are able to hear before they are born; studies show that babies turn toward the sound of their mothers' voices just minutes after being born, indicating they recognize the mother's voice from their time in the womb.

The exception to this rule is vision. A baby's vision changes significantly in the first year of life; initially a baby has a vision range of only 8 – 12 inches and no depth perception. As a result, infants rely primarily on hearing; vision does not become the dominant sense until around the age of twelve months. Babies also prefer faces to other objects. This preference, along with their limited vision range, means that their sight is initially focused on their caregiver.

1. The primary purpose of the passage is to

   a. compare vision in adults to vision in newborns

   b. persuade readers to get their infants' eyes checked

   c. confirm a recent scientific finding about senses

   d. explain how an infant's senses operate and change

2. Vision becomes the dominant sense

   a. at birth

   b. around twelve months of age

   c. when hearing declines

   d. at adulthood

3. Newborns mostly rely on

   a. vision

   b. touch

   c. taste

   d. hearing

4. What is the main idea of this passage?

   a. The senses of babies operate like the senses of adults.

   b. Babies have a limited vision range and rely on hearing for their first months of life.

   c. Babies prefer faces to other objects due to their small range of vision in the early months.

   d. Studies show that babies turn toward the sound of their mothers' voices after being born.

5. What evidence does the author provide to support his claim that babies are able to hear before they are born?

   a. The greatest changes in sensory development happen in the first two years of life.

   b. Vision does not become the dominant sense until around the age of twelve months.

   c. Babies turn toward the sound of their mothers' voices just minutes after being born.

   d. When babies are born, most of their senses operate like those of adults.

In its most basic form, geography is the study of space; more specifically, it studies the physical space of Earth and the ways in which it interacts with, shapes, and is shaped by its habitants. Geographers look at the world from a spatial perspective. This means that at the center of all geographic study is the question *where?* For geographers, the *where* of any interaction, event, or development is a crucial element to understanding it.

This question of *where* can be asked in various fields of study, so there are many subdisciplines of geography. These can be organized into four main categories: (1) regional studies, which examine the characteristics of a particular place; (2) topical studies, which look at a single physical or human feature that impacts the whole world; (3) physical studies, which focus on the physical features of Earth; and (4) human studies, which examine the relationship between human activity and the environment.

6. The subdiscipline of geography that looks at the impact of a single physical or human feature on the world is

   a. regional studies

   b. topical studies

   c. physical studies

   d. human studies

7. Physical studies would most likely examine the

   a. causes of migration during a drought

   b. impact of pollution on human development

   c. height of various mountain ranges around the world

   d. characteristics of a particular region in a country

8. What is the topic of this passage?

   a. human activity

   b. spatial perspective

   c. geography

   d. Earth

9. The center of all geographic study is *where* because

   a. geographers look at the world through a spatial perspective

   b. geography includes the subdiscipline of human studies

   c. it is asked in a variety of fields of study, not just geographic

   d. humans interact with various aspects of their world every day

It could be said that the great battle between the North and South we call the Civil War was a battle for individual identity. The states of the South had their own culture, one based on farming, independence, and the right of both man and state to determine their own paths. Similarly, the North had forged its own identity as a center of centralized commerce and manufacturing. This clash of lifestyles was bound to create tension, and this tension was bound to lead to war. But people who try to sell you this narrative are wrong. The Civil War was not a battle of cultural identities—it was a battle about slavery. All other explanations for the war are either a direct consequence of the South's desire for wealth at the expense of her fellow man or a fanciful invention to cover up this sad portion of our nation's history. And it cannot be denied that this time in our past was very sad indeed.

10. The author believes people say the war was fought because of a clash in cultural identities because they

 a. want to avoid acknowledging the shameful parts of the United States' history

 b. do not believe the Civil War was actually fought between the North and the South

 c. are trying to make a better future for the United States despite its past

 d. hope to promote the cause of the North instead of the South

11. The author believes that the Civil War was fought because of

 a. cultural differences

 b. the South's desire for wealth

 c. slavery

 d. individual identity

12. The topic of the passage is

 a. individual identity

 b. slavery

 c. the cause of the Civil War

 d. desire for wealth

13. The tone of this passage is

 a. hopeful

 b. humorous

 c. cautious

 d. assertive

14. Based on the information from the passage, a person from the North during the time of the Civil War would most likely

 a. work in manufacturing

 b. oppose the Civil War

 c. be a farmer

 d. own slaves

Skin coloration and markings have an important role to play in the world of snakes. Those intricate diamonds, stripes, and swirls help the animals hide from predators, but perhaps most importantly (for us humans, anyway), markings can also indicate whether the snake is venomous. While it might seem <u>counterintuitive</u> for a venomous snake to stand out in bright red or blue, that fancy costume tells any nearby predator that approaching it would be a bad idea.

If you see a flashy-looking snake in the woods, though, those markings don't necessarily mean it's venomous: some snakes have found a way to ward off predators without the actual venom. The scarlet kingsnake, for example, has very similar markings to the venomous coral snake with whom it frequently shares a habitat. However, the kingsnake is actually nonvenomous; it's merely pretending to be dangerous to eat. A predatory hawk or eagle, usually hunting from high in the sky, can't tell the difference between the two species, so the kingsnake gets passed over and lives another day.

15. This passage is primarily about

 a. snake habitats

 b. predators of snakes

 c. snake skin coloration and markings

 d. venomous and nonvenomous snakes

16. The scarlet kingsnake

 a. is venomous to predators

 b. often lives in the same areas as the coral snake

 c. is dangerous to a hawk or eagle

 d. is difficult to eat

17. According to the passage, venomous snakes can

  a. have markings that camouflage them from predators

  b. pretend to be nonvenomous when predators are around

  c. be a threat to nonvenomous snakes

  d. be identified by markings on their skin

18. Based on the passage, *counterintuitive* most likely means

  a. contrary to common belief

  b. similar in meaning

  c. difficult to understand

  d. a wise decision

19. A predatory eagle may pass over a kingsnake because the kingsnake

  a. is venomous

  b. can be easily mistaken for a venomous snake

  c. blends in with its environment

  d. is not as nutritious to the eagle as other snakes

Taking a person's temperature is one of the most basic and common health care tasks. Everyone from nurses to emergency medical technicians to concerned parents should be able to grab a thermometer and take a patient's or loved one's temperature. But what's the best way to get an accurate reading? The answer depends on the situation.

The most common way people measure body temperature is orally. A simple digital or disposable thermometer is placed under the tongue for a few minutes, and the task is done. There are many situations, however, when measuring temperature orally isn't an option. For example, when a person can't breathe through her nose, she won't be able to keep her mouth closed long enough to get an accurate reading. In these situations, it's often preferable to place the thermometer in the rectum or armpit. Using the rectum also has the added benefit of providing a much more accurate reading than other locations can provide.

It's also often the case that certain people, like agitated patients or fussy babies, won't be able to sit still long enough for an accurate reading. In these situations, it's best to use a thermometer that works much more quickly, such as one that measures temperature in the ear or at the temporal artery. No matter which method is chosen, however, it's important to check the average temperature for each region, as it can vary by several degrees.

20. What is the structure of this text?

  a. cause and effect

  b. order and sequence

  c. problem and solution

  d. compare and contrast

21. The most common way to take a temperature is

  a. under the tongue

  b. in the armpit

  c. in the ear

  d. at the temporal artery

22. What is the main idea of this passage?

    a. The best way to take a temperature is by placing the thermometer under the tongue.

    b. Taking a temperature is a very simple task.

    c. Some ways to take a temperature are more beneficial in certain situations.

    d. It is especially difficult to get an accurate temperature reading on children.

23. Why is measuring one's temperature in the ear or at the temporal artery beneficial?

    a. The situation determines the best way to get an accurate temperature reading.

    b. Some patients are not able to sit still long enough for an oral temperature reading.

    c. Everyone should be able to take a patient's or loved one's temperature.

    d. These regions provide a much more accurate reading than other locations.

24. Taking a temperature at the temporal artery

    a. is most accurate when done by a medical doctor

    b. is the best way to get an accurate reading

    c. will result in a different degree reading than from under the tongue

    d. will result in the same degree reading as from the ear

25. According to the text, taking a temperature

    a. is a simple task that most adults should be able to do

    b. can be dangerous if the result is not read correctly

    c. should be left up to medical professionals like nurses

    d. will give consistent results regardless of where it is taken

We've been told for years that the recipe for weight loss is fewer calories in than out. In other words, eat less and exercise more, and your body will take care of the rest. As many who've tried to diet can attest, this <u>edict</u> doesn't always produce results. If you're one of those folks, you might have felt that you just weren't doing it right—that the failure was all your fault.

However, several new studies released this year have suggested that it might not be your fault at all. For example, a study of people who'd lost a high percentage of their body weight (more than 17 percent) in a short period of time found that they could not physically maintain their new weight. Scientists measured their resting metabolic rate and found that they'd need to consume only a few hundred calories a day to meet their metabolic needs. Basically, their bodies were in starvation mode and seemed to desperately hang on to each and every calorie. Eating even a single healthy, well-balanced meal a day would cause these subjects to start packing the pounds back on.

Other studies have shown that factors like intestinal bacteria, distribution of body fat, and hormone levels can affect the manner in which our bodies process calories. There's also the fact that it's actually quite difficult to measure the number of calories consumed during a particular meal and the number used while exercising.

26. This passage is chiefly concerned with

    a. calories

    b. exercise

    c. weight loss

    d. metabolic needs

27. According to the text, hormone levels

    a. can impact a person's ability to lose weight

    b. will change based on a person's diet

    c. make a person think he is losing weight even if he is not

    d. were the subject of a new study released this year

28. Based on the text, *edict* most likely means

    a. hormone

    b. rule

    c. relationship

    d. diet

29. According to the text, people who lose a high percentage of their body weight in a short period of time may

    a. gain more than 17 percent of their body weight back after returning to a normal diet

    b. continue to lose weight if they maintain their normal diet

    c. be susceptible to high levels of intestinal bacteria

    d. start gaining the weight back even with healthy eating habits

30. The author wrote this text to

    a. inform the reader about potential causes of inconsistencies in weight loss

    b. persuade others to practice traditional dieting techniques

    c. warn against losing a high percentage of body weight quickly

    d. compare and contrast the effects of dieting to the effects of exercise

Influenza (also called the flu) has historically been one of the most common, and deadliest, human infections. While many people who contract the virus will recover, many others will not. Over the past 150 years, tens of millions of people have died from the flu, and millions more have been left with lingering complications such as secondary infections.

Although it's a common disease, the flu is not actually highly infectious, meaning it's relatively difficult to contract. The flu can only be transmitted when individuals come into direct contact with bodily fluids of people infected with the flu or when they are exposed to expelled aerosol particles (which result from coughing and sneezing). Because the viruses can only travel short distances as aerosol particles and die within a few hours on hard surfaces, the virus can be contained with fairly simple health measures like hand washing and face masks.

However, the spread of the flu can only be contained when people are aware such measures need to be taken. One of the reasons the flu has historically been so deadly is the amount of time between when people become infectious and when they develop symptoms. Viral shedding—the process by which the body releases viruses that have been successfully reproducing during the infection—takes place two days after infection, while symptoms do not usually develop until the third day of infection. Thus, infected individuals have at least twenty-four hours in which they may unknowingly infect others.

31. The act of releasing viruses that have been reproducing is called

    a. contagious

    b. viral shedding

    c. influenza

    d. aerosol particles

32. The primary purpose of the passage is to

    a. persuade readers to cover their mouths when they cough

    b. argue in favor of the flu vaccine

    c. explain why the flu is so common

    d. inform readers of the symptoms of the flu so it can be identified

33. In this passage, the word *expelled* most likely means

    a. noninfectious

    b. ejected

    c. harmful

    d. hidden

34. Because of the significant amount of time between when people with the flu become infectious and when they develop symptoms,

    a. many infected individuals unknowingly infect others

    b. millions have been left with lingering complications

    c. the infection is not highly contagious

    d. viruses can only travel short distances

35. Based on the passage, the flu virus

    a. can live on hard surfaces for up to two days

    b. is highly infectious and easy to spread to others

    c. has killed tens of millions in the past 150 years

    d. travels long distances as aerosol particles after a sneeze

GENERAL SCIENCE

Read the question, and then choose the most correct answer.

1. The inorganic material that makes up bone is

    a. calcium   b. phosphorus   c. collagen   d. potassium   e. actin

2. An example of a biome is a

    a. beehive   b. cornfield   c. herd of bison   d. desert   e. puddle

3. The planet that is closest to Earth is

    a. Mercury   b. Venus   c. Jupiter   d. Saturn   e. Neptune

4. The phenomenon when a star suddenly increases in brightness and then disappears from view is a(n)

    a. aurora   b. galaxy   c. black hole   d. eclipse   e. supernova

5. Chloroplasts can be found in the cells of

    a. whales   b. mushrooms   c. tulips   d. lizards   e. fish

6. Isotopes of an element will have the same number of

    a. electrons   b. neutrons   c. protons   d. atoms   e. ions

7. An electrocardiogram (EKG) can be used to diagnose

    a. diabetes   b. torn ligaments   c. cancer   d. tachycardia   e. influenza

8. The number of nucleotides in a codon is

    a. 3   b. 4   c. 6   d. 22   e. 64

9. The negatively charged atoms inside an atom are called

    a. protons   b. neutrons   c. electrons   d. ions   e. nucleus

10. A box sliding down a ramp experiences all of the following forces EXCEPT

    a. tension   b. friction   c. gravity   d. normal   e. buoyant

11. An example of an organism that decomposes organic matter is a(n)

    a. apple tree   b. mushroom   c. goat   d. lion   e. vulture

12. An example of an organism that regulates its body temperature externally is a

    a. pelican   b. dolphin   c. whale   d. lobster   e. leopard

13. Which part of the body is affected by a right tibia fracture?

    a. upper arm   b. lower arm   c. upper leg   d. lower leg   e. head

14. The digestive enzymes produced by the pancreas pass into the

    a. stomach   b. gallbladder   c. esophagus   d. large intestine   e. small intestine

15. An example of a physical change is

    a. freezing water   b. baking a cake   c. a rusting fence   d. an exploding firecracker   e. neutralizing an acid

16. A nonrenewable energy source is

    a. water   b. wind   c. coal   d. sunlight   e. geothermal

17. The top layer of the earth's surface is called the

    a. exosphere   b. lithosphere   c. atmosphere   d. biosphere   e. asthenosphere

18. Skeletal muscle is attached to bone by

    a. ligaments   b. cartilage   c. tendons   d. nerves   e. fascia

19. During digestion, food passes through the

    a. esophagus   b. gallbladder   c. trachea   d. pancreas   e. liver

20. The earth rotates on its axis in

    a. one hour   b. one day   c. one month   d. one year   e. one hundred years

21. The process that uses carbon dioxide to produce sugars is called

    a. digestion   b. chloroplast   c. decomposition   d. photosynthesis   e. cellular respiration

22. $2C_6H_{14} + 19O_2 \rightarrow 12CO_2 + 14H_2O$

The reaction shown above is a(n)

a. substitution reaction
b. acid-base reaction
c. decomposition reaction
d. combustion reaction
e. synthesis reaction

23. The abiotic factor in an ecosystem could include

a. producers
b. consumers
c. predators
d. decomposers
e. water

24. In a food web, fungi are

a. producers
b. primary consumers
c. secondary consumers
d. tertiary consumers
e. decomposers

25. The mechanism of evolution is

a. gene flow
b. genetic drift
c. mutation
d. sexual selection
e. natural selection

26. The muscular organ that processes food material into smaller pieces and helps mix it with saliva is the

a. pharynx
b. tongue
c. diaphragm
d. stomach
e. esophagus

27. A strong acid will

a. completely ionize in water
b. donate more than one proton
c. have a pH close to 7
d. not ionize
e. have at least one metal atom

28. The largest bone in the human body is the

a. tibia
b. humerus
c. scapula
d. femur
e. ulna

29. When skin is exposed to the sunlight, it produces

a. vitamin A
b. vitamin E
c. vitamin K
d. vitamin D
e. vitamin B

30. The light reactions of photosynthesis occur in the

a. mitochondria
b. chloroplast
c. cytoplasm
d. vacuole
e. nucleus

31. The exchange of nutrients, gases, and cellular waste happens in the

    a. veins   b. arteries   c. capillaries   d. venules   e. arterioles

32. The incus, stapes, and malleus play an important role in

    a. vision   b. taste   c. hearing   d. smell   e. touch

33. The adrenal glands are located near the

    a. brain   b. thyroid   c. kidneys   d. bladder   e. heart

34. Wind speed is measured using

    a. a thermometer b. a wind vane c. an anemometer d. a rain gauge e. a barometer

35. One milliliter is equivalent to

    a. 1 g   b. 1 pt   c. 1 lb   d. 1 m^2 e. 1 cm^3

36. Mature sperm is stored in the

    a. testes   b. bladder   c. vas deferens   d. epididymis   e. penis

37. The meninges protect the

    a. brain   b. heart   c. stomach   d. uterus   e. testes

38. Organic molecules must contain

    a. carbon   b. phosphorous c. nitrogen   d. oxygen   e. helium

39. DNA and RNA are built from monomers called

    a. amino acids   b. sugars   c. lipids   d. polymerases   e. nucleotides

40. The nucleotide found in RNA but not DNA is

    a. adenine   b. cytosine   c. thymine   d. uracil   e. guanine

41. An organism with 16 total chromosomes will produce gametes with a chromosome number of

    a. 4   b. 8   c. 16   d. 32   e. 64

42. An example of a wedge is a(n)

    a. wagon   b. ramp   c. ax   d. seesaw   e. car axle

43. The number of electrons needed by a noble gas to fill its outermost electron shell is

    a. 0   b. 1   c. 2   d. 3   e. 4

44. Photosynthesis takes place in the

    a. roots   b. stem   c. bark   d. flower   e. leaves

45. The process that occurs when water vapor becomes a solid is

    a. condensation   b. sublimation   c. evaporation   d. deposition   e. freezing

46. Orange juice, which is primarily composed of citric acid and malic acid, likely has a pH of

    a. 4   b. 7   c. 9   d. 13   e. 14

47. The mass of an object is measured with a

    a. thermometer   b. graduated cylinder   c. ruler   d. barometer   e. balance

48. The resistance to motion caused by one object rubbing against another object is

    a. inertia   b. friction   c. velocity   d. gravity   e. acceleration

49. The rock formed when lava cools and solidifies is called

    a. igneous   b. sedimentary   c. metamorphic   d. sandstone   e. mineral

50. An example of a longitudinal wave is a

    a. surface wave   b. light wave   c. sound wave   d. radio wave   e. microwave

51. The gas found in the largest quantity in Earth's atmosphere is

    a. carbon monoxide   b. bromine   c. nitrogen   d. fluorine   e. oxygen

52. All atoms of an element contain the same number of

    a. electrons   b. molecules   c. protons   d. ions   e. neutrons

53. The most common element in the universe is

    a. carbon   b. lithium   c. potassium   d. titanium   e. hydrogen

54. The storm LEAST likely to form over ocean water is a

    a. hurricane   b. typhoon   c. cyclone   d. tornado   e. squall

55. To neutralize an acid spill, use

    a. baking soda   b. lemon juice   c. cat litter   d. water   e. vinegar

56. The force that attracts a body toward the center of the earth is

    a. friction   b. gravity   c. pull   d. tension   e. buoyancy

57. Energy that is stored and is waiting to work is called

    a. kinetic   b. thermal   c. mechanical   d. chemical   e. potential

58. An example of a translucent object is a

    a. book   b. glass of water   c. T-shirt   d. car window   e. door

59. An example of an electrical insulator is a

    a. spoon   b. key   c. marble   d. penny   e. wire

60. Stratus clouds can be described as

    a. often gray   b. big and tall   c. high in the sky   d. puffy   e. usually wispy

VOCATIONAL ADJUSTMENT INDEX

The following statements address certain personal or professional situations. Agreeing or disagreeing with the statements simply reveals how you are likely to think, feel, or act in certain circumstances. If you agree with the statement, select (A) in the corresponding row. If you disagree, select (D). Choose the answer that is most true for you and answer immediately. *Work rapidly.*

1.	People spend too much time focusing on their careers.	1.	(A)	(D)
2.	Most people are too competitive.	2.	(A)	(D)
3.	It is important to be a lifelong learner.	3.	(A)	(D)
4.	Collaboration is key to the success of any organization.	4.	(A)	(D)
5.	Most workplace evaluations are unfair.	5.	(A)	(D)
6.	Most older coworkers are out of touch.	6.	(A)	(D)
7.	People usually have the best intentions.	7.	(A)	(D)
8.	Working with others rather than alone is preferable.	8.	(A)	(D)
9.	It is important to take risks.	9.	(A)	(D)
10.	Efficiency is better than quality.	10.	(A)	(D)
11.	Kind hearts are for weak leaders.	11.	(A)	(D)
12.	A job is just a paycheck.	12.	(A)	(D)
13.	Conflict can be avoided through active listening.	13.	(A)	(D)
14.	Working with others is difficult.	14.	(A)	(D)
15.	Making rules is better than following rules.	15.	(A)	(D)
16.	Most coworkers are helpful.	16.	(A)	(D)
17.	Helping the elderly is rewarding.	17.	(A)	(D)
18.	Multitasking is difficult in collaborative settings.	18.	(A)	(D)
19.	Quiet environments are best for productivity.	19.	(A)	(D)
20.	Happiness is more important than financial stability.	20.	(A)	(D)
21.	You have to work for what you want.	21.	(A)	(D)
22.	Working with children is inspiring.	22.	(A)	(D)
23.	It is acceptable to be selfish in life.	23.	(A)	(D)
24.	Society is overly competitive.	24.	(A)	(D)
25.	Perfection is achievable.	25.	(A)	(D)
26.	An ideal job would be one without a strong workplace culture.	26.	(A)	(D)

27.	It is important to separate business and friendship in the workplace.	27.	Ⓐ	Ⓓ
28.	It is difficult to make new friends.	28.	Ⓐ	Ⓓ
29.	Success is more important than relationships.	29.	Ⓐ	Ⓓ
30.	It is never acceptable to fail or lose.	30.	Ⓐ	Ⓓ
31.	Social events are more exciting than alone time.	31.	Ⓐ	Ⓓ
32.	Most supervisors are compassionate.	32.	Ⓐ	Ⓓ
33.	It is more important to highlight someone's strengths than point out their weaknesses.	33.	Ⓐ	Ⓓ
34.	Being radically candid is important.	34.	Ⓐ	Ⓓ
35.	Unity is much more important than diversity.	35.	Ⓐ	Ⓓ
36.	Most young people are clueless about the world.	36.	Ⓐ	Ⓓ
37.	Everybody has the right to their own opinions.	37.	Ⓐ	Ⓓ
38.	It is better to be vocal than to be submissive.	38.	Ⓐ	Ⓓ
39.	It is better to be respected than feared.	39.	Ⓐ	Ⓓ
40.	The best supervisors know how to delegate tasks to their workers.	40.	Ⓐ	Ⓓ
41.	Seniority is more important than performance.	41.	Ⓐ	Ⓓ
42.	The best workers are self-motivated.	42.	Ⓐ	Ⓓ
43.	Discrimination does not really exist.	43.	Ⓐ	Ⓓ
44.	It is important to make a list of daily tasks.	44.	Ⓐ	Ⓓ
45.	An authority figure should never be contradicted.	45.	Ⓐ	Ⓓ
46.	Some rules are meant to be broken.	46.	Ⓐ	Ⓓ
47.	Employees should be fired if they make a mistake.	47.	Ⓐ	Ⓓ
48.	People who complain are weak.	48.	Ⓐ	Ⓓ
49.	Customers are normally difficult to work with.	49.	Ⓐ	Ⓓ
50.	All leaders should be charismatic.	50.	Ⓐ	Ⓓ
51.	Stress is hard to handle in the workplace.	51.	Ⓐ	Ⓓ
52.	Teamwork is key to organizational success.	52.	Ⓐ	Ⓓ
53.	There is one right path in life and many wrong paths.	53.	Ⓐ	Ⓓ
54.	Money is the root of all evil.	54.	Ⓐ	Ⓓ
55.	All people should be treated with dignity.	55.	Ⓐ	Ⓓ
56.	Friendships with colleagues should be avoided.	56.	Ⓐ	Ⓓ
57.	It feels good to be the center of attention.	57.	Ⓐ	Ⓓ
58.	Most tasks at work are dehumanizing.	58.	Ⓐ	Ⓓ

59.	Employee values should align in the workplace.	59.	(A) (D)
60.	Most jobs consume too much time.	60.	(A) (D)
61.	More elderly people need to retire earlier in life.	61.	(A) (D)
62.	Disagreement is uncomfortable.	62.	(A) (D)
63.	Sacrifice is important for team success.	63.	(A) (D)
64.	Most police officers and security guards are uptight.	64.	(A) (D)
65.	An ideal supervisor would be one who is direct and honest.	65.	(A) (D)
66.	An ideal supervisor would be one who focuses on the details.	66.	(A) (D)
67.	Most people foolishly just follow the rules.	67.	(A) (D)
68.	Customer service is an important part of any job.	68.	(A) (D)
69.	Cheating on an exam is never acceptable.	69.	(A) (D)
70.	Many young people have all the best intentions.	70.	(A) (D)
71.	The most stimulating environments are calm.	71.	(A) (D)
72.	Large events are intimidating.	72.	(A) (D)
73.	Sometimes it is necessary to take an unsanctioned break at work.	73.	(A) (D)
74.	It is easy to reinvent yourself in new environments.	74.	(A) (D)
75.	Conversation with strangers is quite easy.	75.	(A) (D)
76.	Self-created goals are better than those created by others.	76.	(A) (D)
77.	Flexibility is more important than structure.	77.	(A) (D)
78.	Isolated work at a computer is better than collaborative work at a conference table.	78.	(A) (D)
79.	Teachers often cater too much to student needs.	79.	(A) (D)
80.	Variety is necessary for happiness.	80.	(A) (D)
81.	Too many people are looking for a handout in this world.	81.	(A) (D)
82.	People who have trouble choosing a career cannot be trusted as employees.	82.	(A) (D)
83.	People who question norms are more likely to succeed in the workforce.	83.	(A) (D)
84.	Every employee must always be on time, no matter the circumstance.	84.	(A) (D)
85.	Every person deserves access to high-quality medical care.	85.	(A) (D)
86.	It is unfair to break a promise to a colleague.	86.	(A) (D)
87.	It is okay to give up when overwhelmed.	87.	(A) (D)
88.	It is better to lie than hurt someone's feelings.	88.	(A) (D)
89.	Silence is a sign of insecurity.	89.	(A) (D)
90.	A series of smaller projects is preferable to one large project.	90.	(A) (D)

ANSWER KEY

Academic Aptitude: Verbal Skills

1. c.

    Calm means "at ease or peaceful," and the other four words describe the feeling of being upset.

2. e.

    Energetic means "wide awake or perky," and the other four words describe the need for rest.

3. d.

    Certainty means "without a doubt," and the other four words describe issues or situations that need to be solved.

4. b.

    Ordinary means "common or regular," and the other four words mean something strange or extraordinary.

5. c.

    Thrive means "to grow in a positive way," and the other four words describe the inability to grow or the absence of growth.

6. b.

    Thoughtless means "inconsiderate"; the other four words describe someone considerate and caring.

7. c.

    Lacking means "missing or incomplete," and the other four words describe something that is complete or has all its parts.

8. c.

    Bandage means "a covering for an injury," and the other four words are types of injuries.

9. a.

    Lively means "upbeat or energetic," and the other four words refer to something lacking in positive energy.

10. d.

    Long means "lengthy"; the other four words refer to something short or abrupt.

11. e.

    Obvious means "understandable or apparent," and the other four words refer to something unknown, mysterious, or puzzling.

12. b.

    Upbeat means "having a positive attitude," and the other four words refer to having a negative emotional state.

13. e.

    Indifference means "disinterested"; the other four words refer to having an affection or liking for something.

14. e.

    Rude means "showing a lack of manners or consideration," and the other four words refer to being friendly or agreeable.

15. d.

    Divide means to "separate or disconnect," and the other four words refer to joining things together.

16. c.

    Create means "to make something," and the other four words refer to destroying something.

17. b.

    Drip means "trickle or drop," and the other four words refer to a heavy flow—usually of water or blood.

18. c.

    Conflict means "a competition or lack of agreement," and the other four words describe a state of peace or harmony.

19. a.

    Limited means "having defined boundaries," and the other four words refer to something that is never-ending.

20. d.

    Disapprove means "condemn"; the other four words refer to forgiveness or approval.

21. b.

Humility means "modesty"; the other four words refer to being conceited.

22. e.

Perfect means "flawless"; the other four words refer to something flawed or defective.

23. d.

Conceited means "snobbish or arrogant," and the other four words refer to modesty and humbleness.

24. d.

Crude means "vulgar or rude," and the other four words refer to being well mannered.

25. e.

Serious means "thoughtful and sober," and the other four words refer to something ridiculous.

Academic Aptitude: Arithmetic

26. d.

Line up the decimals and add.

$$1.73$$
$$+\ 2.17$$
$$\mathbf{3.90}$$

27. a.

$24.17 + $32.87 = $57.04

$80.00 − $57.04 = **$22.96**

28. b.

Find the highest possible multiple of 4 that is less than or equal to 397, and then subtract to find the remainder.

$99 \times 4 = 396$

$397 − 396 =$ **1**

29. c.

If each student receives 2 notebooks, the teacher will need $16 \times 2 = 32$ notebooks. After handing out the notebooks, she will have 50 − 32 = **18 notebooks left**.

30. a.

Add the number of cupcakes he will give to his friend and to his coworkers, then subtract that value from 48.

# of cupcakes for his friend:

$\frac{1}{2} \times 48 = 24$

# of cupcakes for his coworkers:

$\frac{1}{3} \times 48 = 16$

$48 − (24 + 16) =$ **8**

31. c.

Round each value and add.

$129{,}113 \approx 129{,}000$

$34{,}602 \approx 35{,}000$

$129{,}000 + 35{,}000 =$ **164,000**

32. b.

There are 15 minutes between 7:45 a.m. and 8:00 a.m. and 20 minutes between 8:00 a.m. and 8:20 a.m.

15 minutes + 20 minutes = **35 minutes**

33. c.

$23 \div 4 = 5.75$ pizzas

Round up to **6 pizzas**.

34. e.

Use the formula for finding percentages. Express the percentage as a decimal.

part = *whole* × *percentage* = **1560 × 0.15**

35. b.

Multiply the cost per pound by the number of pounds purchased to find the cost of each fruit.

apples: 2(1.89) = 3.78

oranges: 1.5(2.19) = 3.285

3.78 + 3.285 = 7.065 = **$7.07**

36. c.

Divide 1.3208 by 5.2.

```
        .254
   52) 13.208
       10 4
        2 80
        2 60
          208
          208
            0
```

37. b.

Align the decimals and add/subtract from left to right.

$$17.38 - 19.26 + 14.2$$
$$= (-1.88) + 14.2 = \textbf{12.32}$$

38. e.

Write a proportion and then solve for x.

$$\frac{40}{45} = \frac{265}{x}$$
$$40x = 11{,}925$$
$$x = 298.125 \approx \textbf{298}$$

39. b.

$$\frac{1}{4} = \frac{x}{20}$$
$$4x = 20$$
$$x = \textbf{5}$$

40. c.

$$\frac{25}{2} = \frac{x}{8}$$
$$2x = 200$$
$$x = \textbf{100}$$

41. a.

$$0.8 + 0.49 + 0.89 = 2.18$$
$$2.5 - 2.18 = \textbf{0.32}$$

42. c.

Line up the decimals and subtract.

```
   4.50
 - 1.67
   2.83
```

43. a.

$$\$285.48 \div 6 = \textbf{\$47.58}$$

44. c.

Line up the decimals and subtract.

```
 119.70
 -  1.05
 118.65
```

45. c.

$$\$25.44 \div 3.2 = \textbf{\$7.95}$$

46. a.

$$6.3 \div 18 = \textbf{0.35 lb}$$

47. d.

48 cents = $0.48

$$\$1.68 \div \$0.48 = \textbf{3.5}$$

48. c.

$$127 - 150 = 127 + (-150) = \textbf{-23}$$

49. a.

The average of five numbers is the sum of the numbers divided by 5. Multiply the average by 5 to find the sum; subtract to find the fifth number.

$$\frac{sum}{5} = 16$$
$$sum = 16 \times 5 = 80$$
$$80 - 68 = \textbf{12}$$

50. a.

$$\frac{4}{50} = \frac{x}{175}$$
$$50x = 700$$
$$x = \textbf{14 mL}$$

Academic Aptitude: Nonverbal Skills

51.	b.	**64.**	a.
52.	a.	**65.**	a.
53.	e.	**66.**	b.
54.	a.	**67.**	c.
55.	c.	**68.**	d.
56.	e.	**69.**	a.
57.	d.	**70.**	b.
58.	c.	**71.**	d.
59.	c.	**72.**	b.
60.	a.	**73.**	c.
61.	a.	**74.**	e.
62.	c.	**75.**	c.
63.	e.		

Spelling

1.	a. muscle	**24.**	a. symptom
2.	c. hormone	**25.**	c. eliminate
3.	b. seizure	**26.**	b. adhere
4.	c. facilities	**27.**	b. enable
5.	a. decrease	**28.**	b. various
6.	a. transfusion	**29.**	c. secretion
7.	b. anatomy	**30.**	c. trauma
8.	b. diagnosis	**31.**	c. excessive
9.	c. equipment	**32.**	a. bacteria
10.	a. stomach	**33.**	c. fungus
11.	b. arthritis	**34.**	b. monitor
12.	b. ovary	**35.**	c. abrasion
13.	a. surgical	**36.**	c. multiple
14.	c. allergy	**37.**	a. tremor
15.	a. inflammation	**38.**	c. involvement
16.	c. poison	**39.**	c. respiratory
17.	a. atrophy	**40.**	b. cranial
18.	b. sterile	**41.**	c. disease
19.	a. cellular	**42.**	a. artery
20.	b. tissue	**43.**	b. vein
21.	b. artificial	**44.**	b. chronic
22.	c. immediate	**45.**	c. acute
23.	c. droplet		

Reading Comprehension

1. d.

The passage explains how an infant's senses operate while specifically detailing the changes experienced with vision.

2. b.

The passage states that vision does not become the dominant sense until around the age of twelve months.

3. d.

The passage explains that infants rely primarily on hearing because vision does not become a dominant sense until around the age of twelve months.

4. b.

The passage specifically explains the changes an infant experiences in vision and that because of this late development, hearing is a dominant sense at first.

5. c.

The author explains that studies show that babies turn toward the sound of their mothers' voices just minutes after being born, indicating that an infant recognizes the mother's voice from their time in the womb. This evidence supports the claim that babies are able to hear before they are born.

6. b.

The author states that topical studies look at a single physical or human feature that impacts the whole world.

7. c.

Physical studies focus on the physical features (mountain ranges) of Earth.

8. c.

This passage focuses on geography and its purpose.

9. a.

Geography is the study of space, which means it looks at the world through a spatial perspective, answering the question of *where* something is located.

10. a.

The author says that any explanation for the cause of the Civil War that does not involve slavery is just a fanciful invention to cover up this sad portion of our nation's history. This implies that people do not want to admit something so shameful happened.

11. c.

The author says, "The Civil War was not a battle of cultural identities—it was a battle about slavery."

12. c.

The passage explores proposed causes of the Civil War, which are represented in the other answer choices.

13. d.

The author writes this passage to correct misinformation on the topic of the causes of the Civil War. He writes with an assertive, or self-confident, tone, insisting that his interpretation of this historical event is accurate while the others are wrong. For example, he says, "People who try to sell you this narrative are wrong," showing his confidence in his position and his disdain for others' opinions on this topic.

14. a.

The text explains that the North had "forged its own identity as the center of centralized commerce and manufacturing."

15. c.

This passage explains how the snake's coloration and markings help it hide from predators while also warning humans and predators that it may be venomous.

16. b.

The author explains that the scarlet kingsnake and coral snake frequently share a habitat.

17. d.

The author explains that the markings on a snake can indicate whether a snake is venomous.

18. a.

The text says, "[I]t might seem counterintuitive for a venomous snake to stand out in bright red or blue," meaning that it seems like a venomous snake would want to stay hidden from predators. However, the text continues by explaining that venomous snakes actually can have vivid skin colors and prints to ward off predators, so *counterintuitive* means "contrary to common belief."

19. b.

The author explains that the markings of a kingsnake are very similar to those of a venomous coral snake. The coral snake is dangerous to a predatory eagle, so the eagle avoids eating the kingsnake for fear it is a coral snake.

20. d.

In this text, the various methods of measuring temperatures are being compared and contrasted to answer the question, "What is the best way to get an accurate reading?"

21. a.

The text states that the most common way people take someone's temperature is orally, and the author goes on to clarify that the correct location of the oral thermometer is under the tongue.

22. c.

The article explains the many ways a temperature can be taken. It also tells which methods are most useful and reliable in various situations.

23. b.

The author explains that while taking a temperature orally is most common, many patients are not able to sit still for the length of time it takes to get an accurate reading. Using one's ear or temporal artery is quicker and therefore beneficial in these situations.

24. c.

The author explains that it is important to check the average temperature for each region, as it can vary by several degrees.

25. a.

The first paragraph of the text explains that taking a temperature is a basic medical procedure that can be done by nearly anyone, including a parent.

26. c.

The passage explains weight loss and how each of the other answer choices impact one's ability to lose weight.

27. a.

The text says that hormone levels can affect the manner in which our bodies process calories, which impacts a person's ability to lose weight.

28. b.

The text uses the word *edict* to refer to the commonly understood rule of dieting that says an individual must burn more calories than he or she takes in.

29. d.

The text says that in some cases people who lose a high percentage of their body weight in a short period of time cannot physically maintain their new weight, and as a result, their body will desperately hang on to calories resulting in weight gain even with a healthy diet.

30. a.

The text explains that following a traditional model for calorie intake may not always produce results because of several factors that may interfere with the weight loss process.

31. b.

The process of the body releasing viruses that have been successfully reproducing during the infection is called viral shedding.

32. c.

The topic sentence explains that the flu has historically been one of the most common human infections, and the rest of the passage explains why that is, despite the fact that it is relatively difficult to contract.

33. b.

Because these aerosol particles result from coughing or sneezing, *expelled* means ejected, or forced out.

34. a.

Many infected with the flu unknowingly infect others because their symptoms are undetected for at least twenty-four hours.

35. c.

The passage explains in the first paragraph that the flu is very deadly and has killed tens of millions in the past 150 years.

General Science

1. a.

Calcium is the most abundant mineral found in bones, as well as in the entire body.

2. d.

A biome is a large ecological community that includes specific plants and animals; a desert is one example.

3. b.

Venus's orbit is closest to Earth. Venus is the second planet from the sun, and Earth is the third planet from the sun.

4. e.

Before a star collapses, the star burns brighter for a period of time and then fades from view. This is a supernova.

5. c.

Tulips are plants, meaning they have chloroplasts to perform photosynthesis.

6. c.

Isotopes are atoms of the same element with the same number of protons but different numbers of neutrons.

7. d.

Tachycardia is an abnormally fast heart rate, and electrocardiograms show the electrical activity of the heart.

8. a.

Each codon contains three nucleotides.

9. c.

Electrons are negatively charged particles in an atom; electrons orbit the nucleus.

10. a.

Tension is the force that results from objects being pulled or hung.

11. b.

Mushrooms are fungi. Fungi break down organic material left by dead animals and plants, making them decomposers.

12. d.

The metabolic rate of crustaceans, such as lobsters, is too low to regulate their temperature. Crustaceans use behavioral techniques, such as moving to shallow water, to maintain body temperature.

13. d.

The tibia is a lower leg bone.

14. e.

The digestive enzymes produced by the pancreas pass into the small intestine.

15. a.

When water changes form, it does not change the chemical composition of the substance. Once water becomes ice, the ice can easily turn back into water.

16. c.

Coal is nonrenewable because once coal is burned, it cannot be quickly replaced.

17. b.

The lithosphere is the top layer of the earth's surface.

18. c.

The skeletal muscles and the bone are attached by the tendons.

19. a.

The esophagus is the muscular passageway through which food travels on its way from the mouth to the stomach.

20. b.

Earth takes approximately twenty-four hours to rotate on its axis.

21. d.

Photosynthesis is the process by which plants convert the energy of the sun into stored chemical energy (glucose).

22. d.

Combustion is defined as a reaction in which a hydrocarbon reacts with O_2 to produce CO_2 and H_2O.

23. e.

Nonliving things in an ecosystem, like air and water, are abiotic factors.

24. e.

Most fungi derive their energy by breaking down dead plant and animal matter.

25. e.

The mechanism of natural selection is rooted in the idea that there is variation in inherited traits among a population of organisms, resulting in differential reproduction.

26. b.

The tongue is the muscle that helps break apart food, mix it with saliva, and direct it toward the esophagus.

27. a.

When placed in water, strong acids immediately break apart into their constituent ions.

28. d.

The femur is the largest bone of the human body.

29. d.

Sunlight helps the skin produce vitamin D.

30. b.

The light reactions of photosynthesis occur in the chloroplast. Each chloroplast has stacks of membranes called thylakoids where enzymes convert light energy into chemical energy.

31. c.

Capillaries enable exchange of cellular waste, gases, and nutrients on the cellular level.

32. c.

The incus, stapes, and malleus are bones connected to the skull that play an important role in the sense of hearing.

33. c.

Adrenal glands sit on top of each kidney.

34. c.

An anemometer measures wind speed.

35. e.

$1 \text{ ml} = 1 \text{ cm}^3$

36. d.

Mature sperm are stored in the epididymis.

37. a.

Meninges are present only in the dorsal cavity that holds the spinal cord and brain.

38. a.

Organic compounds may contain phosphorous, nitrogen, or oxygen, but they *must* contain carbon.

39. e.

Nucleic acids (DNA and RNA) are composed of nucleotides. Each nucleotide is composed of a five-carbon sugar, a nitrogenous base, and a phosphate group.

40. d.

Uracil is found in RNA but not in DNA.

41. b.

Gametes (sperm and egg) have half the number of chromosomes contained in an organism's somatic cells.

42. c.

An ax is an example of a wedge.

43. a.

The valence shell of the noble gases (group 18) is full, so these gases do not need to add electrons.

44. e.

Through photosynthesis, leaves use the sun's energy to convert carbon dioxide into glucose.

45. d.

Deposition occurs when a gas becomes a solid.

46. a.

Acids have a pH between 0 and 7.

47. e.

A balance measures mass.

48. b.

Friction occurs when motion is impeded because one object is rubbing against another object.

49. a.

Igneous rocks form when liquid rock cools and solidifies.

50. c.

Sound waves are longitudinal waves because the vibrations travel in the same direction as the energy.

51. c.

Nitrogen makes up 78 percent of Earth's atmosphere.

52. c.

All atoms of the same element contain the same number of protons.

53. e.

Hydrogen is the most common element in the universe.

54. d.

Tornadoes occur when warm air masses collide with cold air masses over land.

55. a.

Baking soda (sodium bicarbonate) is a base, which will neutralize an acid.

56. b.

Gravity is a force that attracts objects to the center of the earth or toward other objects having mass.

57. e.

Potential energy is energy that is stored and waiting to work.

58. c.

A T-shirt is translucent; it lets some light pass through.

59. c.

A marble is an example of an electrical insulator—it stops the transfer of electrical energy. The other choices are all electrical conductors.

60. a.

Stratus clouds are often gray.

Vocational Adjustment Index

There is no "right" answer to the questions on the Vocational Adjustment Index. Every school will interpret your score differently, so just focus on answering the questions quickly and honestly.

Follow the link below to take your second PSB HOAE practice test:

www.ascenciatestprep.com/psb-hoae-online-resources

R
697
.A4
A83
2018

**PSB health occupations
study guide**